Healthy Clergy Makes Healthy Congregations

A COMPANY OF PASTORS - OVERCOMING THE ISOLATION OF THE PASTORATE

Healthy Clergy Makes Healthy Congregations

A COMPANY OF PASTORS – OVERCOMING THE ISOLATION OF THE PASTORATE

STEPHEN McCUTCHAN

PRIMIX
PUBLISHING
THE WRITE CHOICE

Primix Publishing
East Brunswick Office Evolution
1 Tower Center Boulevard, Ste 1510
East Brunswick, NJ 08816
www.primixpublishing.com
Phone: 1-800-538-5788

Published by Primix Publishing: 10/10/2024

ISBN: 979-8-89194-102-1(sc)
ISBN: 979-8-89194-103-8(e)

Library of Congress Control Number: 2024901982

Contents

This book is dedicated to all the brave souls who have heard God's call to the ministry.

Like Abraham and Sarah, we set off on a journey trusting that God knows where we are going.

Clergy dare to proclaim that forgiveness is more powerful than revenge, generosity wiser than greed, love triumphs over hate, faithfulness more essential than winning, and that grace can transform the worst sin into God's saving strategy.

We know that we are far from perfect, but we dare to believe what God said to Paul, "My grace is sufficient for you, for my power is made perfect in weakness" (2 Corinthians 12:9.

I salute all of you.

IN APPRECIATION

While any errors in this book are my responsibility, there are far fewer of them because of the skilled editing by my wife Sandy. Her eye for both the missing comma and the confusing sentence as well as her enormous patience and support have encouraged me to risk self-publishing as the route to deliver my efforts in the care of clergy.

I'm also grateful to my daughter, Nicole, and Christine Kaposztas who contributed their design skills and computer knowledge to the creation of the cover for the books in the *Healthy Clergy Make Healthy Congregations* (HCMHC) series.

Thanks also to my beta readers: Walter Smith, Nathan Brooks, Jill Crainshaw, Martha Stevenson, Jim Splitt, and William Hull. This book is improved because of your suggestions.

CALLED BY GOD

When in doubt my steps

Begin to slow

And I question what I do

Or what I know

Then from heaven I sense a smile

And a chuckle from eternity all the while

As a word or act interrupts my space

With just the needed glimpse of grace

Steve McCutchan

INTRODUCTION

This book offers a fresh approach to being part of "a company of pastors." Many clergy have discovered the value of being part of some form of pastoral support group. Many judicatories have encouraged such support groups as a counterpoint to the problem of isolation and loneliness in the pastoral ministry.

The format of such groups varies. Often they are informal groups that gather on an infrequent basis for lunch and conversation. Sometimes they have a more regular meeting time, say once a month, and either discuss the lectionary passages in preparation for preaching or participate in a Bible study together. Occasionally, especially if supported by a judicatory, they may invite some professional leadership to moderate the group, make use of a case study model, or deliberately focus on particular issues faced by members of the group. Many times they are denominationally specific but at other times they are ecumenical or even interfaith in nature. During forty years in the ministry, the author has been part of all of these groups, and each has had its benefit.

Since I believe that a major challenge to maintaining our health as clergy is the factor of clergy isolation and the type of loneliness inherent in our profession, this book offers another resource in support of "a company of pastors." As will be explained further, I suggest that the group make use of stories as a means of exploring the various aspects of clergy life. By using fictional tales of clergy, the participants can explore the general challenge of ministry before turning to the more specific experiences of their own lives. At least as a beginning, I am providing three volumes of *Clergy Tales—Tails* as a resource for these gatherings. They may be accessed electronically on Amazon or my Web site *www.smccutchan.com*. All three volumes are offered in a printed form in a single volume as part of the *Healthy Clergy Make Healthy Congregations* series.

I am ordained in the Presbyterian Church (USA) but believe that the approach offered addresses an issue that is found in the lives of clergy in all denominations and independent churches. Occasionally you may need to translate my terminology of presbytery, session, elders, etc. to the parallel terminology in your particular tradition.

As will be seen in the design that follows, I believe that we need to draw upon the spiritual resources that are part of our profession. If your particular group includes clergy of other faiths—a rabbi, an imam, etc.—you should have an honest conversation ahead of time with them about what types of spiritual practices within the group will be appropriate. Sometimes such a group agrees upon certain common practices such as times of silence. At other times, each is invited to bring to the group their specific tradition as a means of enriching the entire group. You will discover that the stresses, challenges, conflicts, and emotional pressures of clergy are shared across traditions, and we are often encouraged by such awareness that we can be of support to each other.

If your group is familiar with the *Revised Common Lectionary*, you may find my *Water Series* on the lectionary to be useful, either as part of your meetings or as a resource for the members of the group between meetings. This lectionary series offers theological reflections on each of the passages of the lectionary for the three-year cycle. While the reflections may be useful in sermon preparation, the intent is to provide theological reflection that can feed the pastor's soul even with passages that are not used in your sermons. Each volume offers five formats for personal prayer experiences based on the five elements of worship—

praise, confession, thanksgiving, intercession, and benediction—so that a pastor can have a time of prayer each of the five days of the week leading up to the worship experience on Sunday. These volumes, and all of my publications in support of clergy, are available on Amazon. You may review all of the resources on my Web site *www.smccutchan.com.*

The first part of this book is particularly addressed to those who have a responsibility for the care of other clergy in their tradition. These may be judicatory officials, members of a pastoral care task force, or a clergy counseling center. In this age of budgetary realities that necessitate staff reduction together with the fractional nature of our society, many people in these positions are overwhelmed with addressing critical conditions and yearn for a way to be proactive in preventing problems. This book offers an approach that can make use of a variety of forms of leadership.

If you are already part of a support group and just want to enrich your experience, this part of the book may not be as important as the more specific design proposed in the next chapters.

As you build your "company of pastors," there are a couple of categories of clergy that you are invited to consider. We have been focusing on those who are called to be pastors of churches. In addition, there are at least two other categories of those called that might enrich your meetings.

First, look around your congregations and community and consider those who have retired from active ministry. There are a variety of ways that clergy live out their retirement. Some become totally inactive while others seek new forms of ministry or become a supportive associate to overworked pastors.

Some enjoy being interim pastors and applying the wisdom drawn from years in the ministry to assisting a church in between clergy. Others enjoy temporary preaching assignments or offering pastoral visits on behalf of a church. Some, like me, enjoy the freedom to focus on various writing projects. We are still pastors responding to God's call in our life, but now the call has become more focused.

If you can identify and invite one or two retired pastors to participate, you will find that they can bring to your conversation a rich body of experience. Of course, you need to be selective in such an invitation and identify retired pastors who have a reputation for drawing wisdom from their experience. Your focus is not to hear a series of old "war stories," but it is useful to balance current experiences with those that occurred earlier in the church.

The second category for your consideration are those who are identified as having entered into specialized ministry. While not serving in a pastorate, they have been theologically trained and in most cases have been ordained within their particular denomination but choose to exercise their gifts in some form of ministry other than that of the congregation.

Some exercise their ministry in the familiar structures of chaplaincy or counseling ministry. Others work in social service agencies that minister to the poor or needy in our society. Still others find their calling in law, medicine, business, etc. All understand themselves as practicing their calling.

Like the retired pastors, people who have experienced ministry in other forms can bring a fresh perspective to some of the issues you will be discussing.

If your continuing group is drawn from those currently serving churches, you may decide to have a special meeting or two in which inviting some who serve in a different category can enrich your experience.

FREQUENCY OF MEETINGS

Your particular group will need to determine the frequency of your meetings. Once a month will not overburden a pastor's schedule but will be frequent enough to provide continuity of experience. As the group becomes acquainted, they may well choose to have some additional meetings. Occasional social events with spouses, seeing movies together, going to sporting events, etc. can strengthen the bonds among your colleagues.

As will be mentioned, I encourage the group to draw upon the spiritual resources that undergird their respective calls. While, as part of the Reformed tradition, I believe that God's call comes to all of us, I am especially concerned by that unique call that clergy experience. I will introduce some psalms and other Scripture resources adapted to speak directly to the particular calling of clergy. You should feel free to adapt them as befits the group.

Also there will be exercises, litanies, and other activities that you can freely copy to share with the group. All members of the group need copies of the short stories and the novel for themselves.

I intend to produce other short stories, novels, etc. that you may want to draw upon for future discussions. If you are interested in being informed of these new resources, please send a request by email to steve@smccutchan.com. Feedback on your experience, including a review on Amazon, will also be appreciated.

Thanks for all you do to support each other in the ministry. Even with all the stresses and strains of the calling, may you experience a deep satisfaction in being part of a great journey.

CHAPTER 1

CLERGY NEED EACH OTHER

SWIMMING AGAINST THE STREAM

You are called by God to offer ministry in this real world. Regardless of your theological perspective, you can resonate with the theological description that we live in a "sin-filled world." To paraphrase Reinhold Niebuhr, one of the few theological doctrines that is experientially verifiable is the "total depravity of humanity." Even those whose emphasis in their ministry is some version of the "power of positive thinking" recognize that we are swimming against the tide. For Christians, the central theme of Jesus' ministry from beginning to end is a confrontation with the brokenness of the world. It begins in violence when Herod seeks to kill him and ends on the cross. The cross represents the summary of the world's response to God's gracious gift of love and grace. Yes, the resurrection demonstrates that no sin, however horrible, can defeat God, but Jesus' life demonstrates that even the most faithful cannot escape the violence of our broken world.

JESUS' MODEL OF COMMUNITY

Continuing with the life of Jesus as the model for our ministry, one of Jesus' first acts of ministry was to call several disciples to accompany

1

him in ministry. There is no justification in the description we have of Jesus' ministry in the Gospels for us to attempt to be the proverbial "Lone Ranger" in our ministry. When we look at the behavior of the disciples, with all of their misunderstandings and mistakes, we cannot even defend our solo act on the basis that others do not have the proper theology or behavior. While the Genesis creation story is speaking of all humanity when God said "It is not good for the [human] to be alone," it applies doubly to the vocation of clergy. John Calvin recognized this when he formed a "company of pastors" as part of his development of the church in Geneva.

THE LONELINESS OF MINISTRY

Across denominations there appears to be a consensus that one of the major challenges facing pastors is the issue of clergy isolation. Sometimes by choice, at other times because of geography or other barriers, clergy experience loneliness and/or isolation as they exercise their ministry. Many times when a pastor does get in trouble, a contributing factor is the isolation of the pastor from others who can help him or her process what is happening. Clergy are surrounded by people, but very few who truly understand the complexity of ministry and the pressures that clergy experience.

Among their clergy colleagues, they often lack the bonds of trust that allow them to probe the depth of what they are experiencing. For a variety of reasons ranging from ego, competition, theological differences, jealousy, time constraints, geography, and exhaustion, many clergy rarely have "a company of pastors" with whom they can truly share.

CLERGY NEED EACH OTHER

Those responsible for the support of clergy have sought creative ways
to offer clergy support groups to counteract the toxic effect of clergy
isolation. This book offers another approach for clergy support groups
to augment the efforts that people are making. We need each other as
we seek to be faithful to our call to ministry.

BUILDING A COMPANY OF PASTORS

Here is the challenge. Judicatory staffs feel overwhelmed by the task
before them. Budget cuts have reduced their staff. The anxiety of our age
is causing a lot of fracturing and faultfinding in our society. Judicatory
personel spend a lot of time just putting out fires.

Most clergy would agree that we need to support each other, but the
trust level among clergy is at a low point, and the demands of the
profession leave them reluctant to commit to one more energy-sapping
meeting that holds little promise. So the task is to find a way to build
a community among pastors that does several things at once:

1. The effort cannot require a large expenditure of energy
   from already stressed judicatory staff.

2. It must offer an opportunity to build good friendships.

3. It must be enjoyable so as to lift the spirits of the tired and
   dispirited.

4. It must be held at a time that is often flexible in a pastor's
   schedule.

5. It must be consistent with the faith that has shaped us.

EXPLORING POSSIBILITIES

While there is no easy solution to that challenge, this book offers you a creative alternative. I will speak of presbyteries, but this can apply equally to diocese, associations, districts, etc.

First, I would suggest that judicatory staff follow God's advice to Moses, Exodus 18, and select some individuals that might assist in making this a reality. Look at your presbytery and identify three or four pastors that you think are held in respect and have some influence with others. Speak to them about the challenge and ask if they would be willing to issue the invitation to seven to ten pastors to gather for some food, fun, and fellowship. The focus would be to explore a fresh approach to becoming a clergy support group.

Particularly if there are few churches of the same denomination in the area, an ecumenical gathering might be considered. Such a possibility would be strengthened if the judicatory personnel of the different traditions were consulted and in support of the gathering.

LOCATION, LOCATION, LOCATION

It is best if the gathering not be during the day because that feels too much like a meeting. A home atmosphere would be excellent. Depending on the group, another possibility might be a reserved room at a restaurant. What you want is to create a relaxed social atmosphere. These are friends getting together to unwind and enjoy each other after a hard week's work.

Food and beverage helps build the social atmosphere. However, if it is at a home, the food should be simple. Subways can make a simple but excellent meal. If possible, at least at the first meeting, the food and drink are provided. The arrangement allows for easy conversation and encourages easy exchange and visibility among all participants. Long rectangular tables are not good for conversation.

The leader makes the agenda clear from the beginning. You are seeking to nurture bonds of trust that enable pastors to encourage and support each other in ministry. You want to explore how "a company of pastors" might both strengthen each other's spirits and offer some joy in life.

There are both advantages and disadvantages to stepping beyond the boundaries of denominational identity. A strong ecumenical or even interfaith support group has the additional benefit of countering the public image of religious fights that seem to contradict the underlying principles of our faith. From experience, I can tell you that a rabbi or imam experience many similar stresses that are experienced by the clergy. However, they need to be aware that the initial stories will be drawn from a Christian context.

In some cases, the isolation is the result of geographical challenges. Whether it be a rural parish many miles from colleagues or just the traffic problems of traveling across a metropolitan area, it is not always easy to bring a group together. If distance is a barrier to late afternoon or early evening meetings, one of the techno geeks among you might assist in setting up something like a Google hangout or Go To Meeting connection. While face-to-face meetings are important for building community, they might be interspersed with these technological forms of meetings. This would also allow judicatory staff to drop in on such meetings occasionally and make their support visible.

MEETING ONE

WHAT DO ALL PASTORS
SHARE IN COMMON?

A SHARED REALITY

This first meeting of your exploratory "company of pastors" is critical. It is important to establish some unique aspects of being a pastor that are shared by clergy across a large spectrum from large church to small church, conservative to liberal, male and female, young and old. What is it that you all share as clergy?

After all have arrived and been welcomed, begin by asking all present to:

1. Introduce himself or herself.

2. Share a brief statement about his or her particular ministry.

3. Complete the statement:"One thing each of us share is . . ."

It is important from the beginning that all are asked to share. You do not want a group in which two or three dominate the conversation. After you have heard each person share their statement, you may find it important for the group to discuss what they have heard.

A GENUINE COMMUNITY OF TRUST

The leader might then share that s/he has been asked to convene the group to explore the viability of participating in a "company of pastors." If this is not a Presbyterian group or is an interfaith gathering, you might want to choose a descriptive title that is more inclusive. You can explain that the origin of the term "a company of pastors" is from the works of John Calvin and then invite the group to alter the title if so desired.

Ask those gathered to reflect together on how it might affect each of their ministries if they regularly met with a small group of clergy whom they can trust and who genuinely care about the obstacles each encounters. As part of their deliberation, invite them to enter into ten minutes of silent prayer contemplating that question. At the end of that time, each will be asked to share two statements of the benefit of such an experience and one possible barrier they would need to overcome if that were to be a reality.

HOW WE BEGIN

Your proposal is to begin with a commitment to meeting together once a month with a variety of experiences designed to build trust and encourage mutual support in their respective ministries. At least initially, the gatherings will include food, be in an informal setting, offer a variety of possibilities for sharing, and recognize the commonality that we share as clergy.

Ask each of them to share their initial response to such a proposal. Would they be willing to commit to six meetings, once a month, and then decide on their future as a group? Tell them they can discuss that possibility together, but then each person will be asked to communicate their personal decision to the leader by the end of the following week.

A POLL OF PRESBYTERY EXECUTIVES

As a conclusion, share with them that a recent poll of presbytery executives resulted in a consensus that one of the great challenges for contemporary pastors was the issue of isolation and loneliness. When the group meets the next time, they will be provided a document that examines the aspects of clergy life that contributes to such loneliness as a basis for discussion.

Identify with them a potential time and place for those who agree to become part of this "company of pastors."

MEETING TWO

SHARED LONELINESS OF PASTORS

One of the challenges in building a group among clergy is to help them understand that there are others who understand the complex nature of ministry whom they can trust. The focus of this meeting is to help clergy discover a shared bond among themselves that transcends any theological or social convictions that often create tension among clergy.

All meetings should begin with an opportunity to socialize and catch up with each other as well as prayer or a spiritual exercise appropriate to the group. Then you introduce the "loneliness exercise." (You have permission to make copies of the various exercises throughout the book.) You are asking them to examine the document and identify at least four areas that most speak to their personal experience.

AN EXAMINATION OF LONELINESS

Do you ever wonder why being a pastor is such a lonely calling? Numerous people surround you. Many of those people both like and admire you. You have the privilege of being present at some of the tenderest and most intimate moments in people's lives. You experience great satisfaction in being able to contribute to people's lives. Still, you experience significant moments of loneliness.

The source of loneliness will vary in intensity and cause for different pastors. It is difficult to explain to outsiders, but most pastors know loneliness. For many pastors, it is just a dull ache, but occasionally that loneliness has a toxic effect that needs to be guarded against. Look at your own life and choose at least four reasons from the list below as prime sources for your own experience of loneliness—there may be more.

WHEN I REFLECT ON MY MINISTRY

1. I am entrusted with painful secrets of members for which there are no easy answers, but I cannot share these secrets with anyone else.

2. Society's image of success requires paying too much attention to people's immediate desires and not enough to their profound needs.

3. I feel guilty that I cannot meet my family's needs and the multiple expectations of the congregation—many of which are quite legitimate on both sides.

4. If a conflict arises between me and a prominent member of the church, my governing board is reluctant to intervene and expects me to cope on my own.

5. I work 60 to 70 hours each week trying to meet the needs of the congregation, but I hear more complaints than appreciation for my efforts.

6. It is hard to stay in touch with the vision of God's call when I am overwhelmed by the often petty and certainly tedious daily grind of pastoral life.

7. I know many people, but I do not have many really good friends—good friendship requires more time than I have available given the demands of the church.

8. The Gospel calls me to boldness, but I feel paralyzed by fear of discord in the congregation.

9. The public images of religious hypocrisies and embarrassing church scandals make me embarrassed to tell others what I do. How can I take pride in my profession?

10. I grieve over the losses I see in a congregation because of death, tragedy, or conflict. Few people understand the pain I feel in such situations.

While all of these causes may be relevant to some degree, which four would be most significant for you?

FOUR AREAS OF LONELINESS

After time to complete the exercise, ask each person to share their four chosen areas with no more than a sentence or two of explanation for each. When all have shared their chosen areas, have a general discussion about what they have heard.

There is no shame in feeling the pain of loneliness in our profession. In fact the better pastor we are, the more we will absorb the pain in other people's lives and be sensitive to the deeply fractured nature of our society. However, it is important to discover ways that we can process these feelings and not allow them to become toxic in our lives.

"A Company of Pastors" may be one opportunity.

Next, begin to explore some of the general ways in which each has discovered practices, techniques, etc. that help him or her cope with the reality of the profession.

After that general discussion, introduce the possibility of making use of stories as a stimulus for their discussion among themselves. Explain that the author, Stephen McCutchan, has created a series of stories about clergy life to facilitate such a discussion. It is his thesis that such stories, like parables, can enable clergy to enjoy an introduction to various issues as they begin to examine both the obstacles and satisfactions that we experience in ministry.

As a way to explore this idea, you will suggest that they obtain a copy of Volume 1 of *Clergy Tales—Tails: Who Wags the Dog?* at Amazon. The link is *amzn.to/11j6L2D.* An electronic version of the volume currently costs 99 cents. If they do not have a Kindle, Amazon offers a free Kindle App that allows them to read the book on a smart phone, notebook, or computer. All three volumes have been combined into one printed book available at *www.smccutchan.com.*

Ask the participants to read "Never Off the Clock" for your next meeting.

MEETING THREE

Never Off the Clock

GUIDING THE DISCUSSION

E-mail all the participants several days before you meet and remind them that they are to download the book and read the short story "Never Off the Clock" before they meet. Provide them the link *amzn. to/11j6L2D* and remind them that Amazon offers a free download of a Kindle App so that they can use whatever device they have. This may not be necessary, depending on the members of your group, but since the story is very short, you might want to have a couple of iPads or notebooks available on which the book is downloaded just in case someone comes but has not read the story. This would also allow people to reference certain passages during the discussion.

Since a major objective of these experiences is to build relationships, always allow plenty of time to check in with each other and to share in some simple food and beverage. While the discussion is an essential part of the group experience, it should be far more than a study group. Be flexible in case something important arises that needs to be shared. It would also be good to establish a practice of including some liturgical act in your meetings together. I will, from time to time, include a liturgical exercise that you are free to copy and use with the group. I would appreciate it if you would attach my name and Web site to the exercise so that people who are interested may be able to contact me.

If any of these subjects stimulates a lengthy discussion, always be prepared to suggest that the discussion be continued at the next meeting.

"Never Off the Clock" builds on the feelings that can be generated by a combination of loneliness and exhaustion raised in the last meeting. The questions provided are to help you facilitate the discussion.

REFLECTIONS ON NEVER OFF THE CLOCK

As the story begins, the pastor reflects on the demanding day that he has experienced. Note how the events quickly move up and down like a roller coaster. Bulletins must be prepared, budget anxieties dealt with, meetings are not always satisfying, people do criticize—not always fairly, and at other times you are able to offer nurture in hospitals and support to those in need of counseling. Allow the group to discuss how realistic that picture is of the rhythm of ministry.

In addition to alcohol, what are some other unhealthy ways in which clergy occasionally succumb at points of either physical or emotional exhaustion?

What are some healthy ways that people have discovered to cope with the emotional drain of ministry?

Picture yourself offering counsel to a new minister on how to cope with the reality of being subject to calls any time day or night. What would you want to say?

If you could make one change in the way you respond to the demands of ministry that sometimes drain you emotionally and spiritually, what would that change be?

Bring the discussion to a close while there is still good energy in the room. Ask them for any evaluation of the process so far. Suggest that the other story in Volume 1, "Your Brother's Blood" will be the focus of the discussion next time. Also ask them to look at the other suggested resources at the end of *Clergy Tales—Tails: Who Wags the Dog* as potential material for the future.

Be sure to establish the time and place for meeting number four.

MEETING FOUR

Your Brother's Blood

WELCOME AND CATCHING UP

Each time you gather there should be ample time to check in with each other. The purpose of the group is to build a set of trusting relationships in which clergy feel supported and nourished.

Also ask them if there were any questions or insights as a result of the last meeting that someone would like to mention. Sometimes an issue will arise that takes precedence over the planned discussion.

When it seems appropriate, the discussion can begin on "Your Brother's Blood." People may want to share some general responses before you begin to focus on particular issues raised by the story.

REFLECTIONS ON "YOUR BROTHER'S BLOOD"

1. In the story, Carla shares her feelings of anger at how easily people can ignore the pain of those who suffer in the world. In response, Al says:

"As a pastor, I see people's capacity to shield themselves from other people's pain all the time. To be honest, I do that myself sometimes."

What are some of the tactics that people, including clergy, make use of to shield themselves from the pain of the world?

2. When Carla asks how people will respond at the presbytery meeting, Al responds:

"To be honest…I think they will admire your courage, be touched by your stories, and be afraid to take any significant action that might upset the people in their congregations."

He then proceeds to speak about the pressures to compromise that pastors feel:

"I know it sounds defensive, but these pastors are not bad people, Carla. Most pastors I know genuinely want to be faithful and respond to human need, but they feel a lot of pressure to compromise when it comes to speaking out."

Whether it is this type of issue or something else, how often do you think pastors feel a tension between what they want to say and do and what they feel the members of their congregation will accept? Give some general examples that you think affect many pastors?

3. Carla describes her sense of God's call as being based on seeing the courage of Caesar Chavez and wanting that type of courage of faith. Al then speaks of the sense of dignity he derived as an insecure young person from feeling called by God. How would you describe your original sense of call and its effect on you?

4. When speaking of the challenge of ministry, Al speaks of people's fear of change and uses the Genesis' image of God placing a dome over the chaos of the waters to protect people from being overwhelmed but still allowing some water or chaos into peoples' lives. Then he says:

"Many people in our congregations want to be merciful but only if it doesn't change things too much. They want to cling to the order in society that benefits them—hide under their self-constructed dome. These are the people who pay the pastor's salary, and, maybe even more important, these are the people who are the pastor's friends."

How realistic do you think fear of change is in congregations? How would you describe the pressure it places on pastors?

5. Al tries to describe the effect of the compromises forced on pastors in ministry:

"I do not know many pastors who do not, at some level, feel they compromise their souls in the very act of being in the ministry."

Then he uses the analogy of a love relationship that grows cold:

"A pastor falls in love with a people," said Al. "At first the pastor thinks the relationship is made in heaven and wants to do things to please them. Then their constant demands begin to chip away at the pastor's passion. He or she feels more used than loved."

In what way does a pastor sometimes feel s/he compromises the faith as s/he responds to the needs that arise in the ministry? What are some ways pastors can avoid having their passion for ministry drain away?

6. The strategy that Al and Carla developed for her presentation at presbytery was to encourage people to remember both their sense of call and God who has called them. How does it impact you when, even in times of great stress, you remember that it is God who has called you to your ministry?

7. What are the ways that you keep in touch with your sense of God's call in your life?

8. Stepping aside from the specific issue of immigration for the moment, what issues does this story lift up for you with respect to your experience of ministry?

9. Is there anything else from the story that you would like to discuss?

Inform the group that in place of a new story for next time, they will engage in an exercise that examines what is meant by "healthy and unhealthy clergy."

MEETING FIVE

WHAT IS MEANT BY UNHEALTHY CLERGY?

WHAT DO HEALTHY CLERGY LOOK LIKE?

You may have read some of the recent articles concerning the declining health of clergy. While the Duke Health Initiative may be the most extensive study, many other groups have done studies that have similar results. Ask the group to describe the difference between a healthy clergy and an unhealthy clergy? What is the image they have of each?

RATE YOUR OWN LEVEL OF HEALTH

Both healthy and unhealthy clergy experience stress and challenges. The difference is how they respond to life's circumstances. Explain that you are going to share with them an exercise that graphs the distinction between unhealthy clergy (UC) and healthy clergy (HC) on a continuum. None of us is completely healthy. All of us do better in some areas than others.

Pass out copies of the "Twenty Areas of Contrast." Explain that on a continuum with Unhealthy Clergy on one end and Healthy Clergy on the other, participants are asked to rate themselves from 1 (UC) to 100 (HC). This is a self-evaluation rather than a judgment.

Once they have rated themselves in each of the twenty areas, have them create a simple graph with the twenty categories on the horizontal line and lines representing units of 10 to 100 on the vertical line.

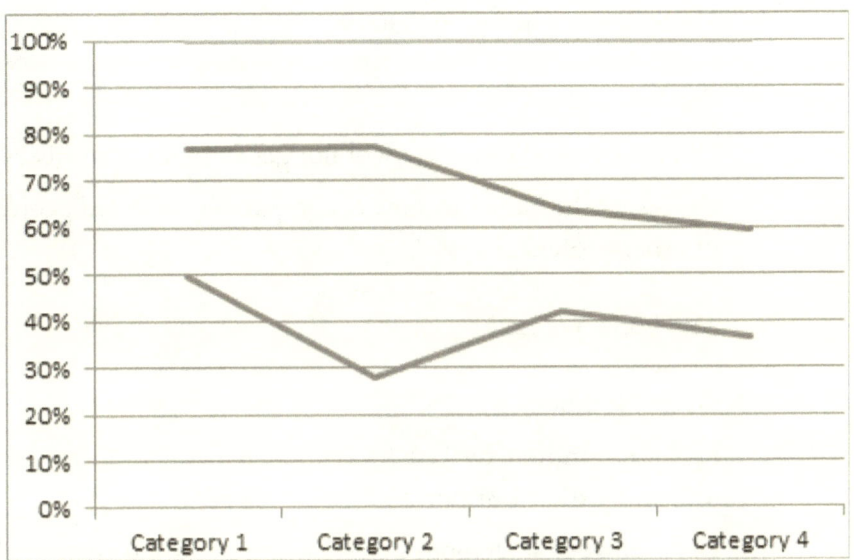

Once they have graphed their responses, they can identify areas where they would like to raise their scores. Suggest that they first look at an easy area where s/he might improve. Then pick a more difficult area and try to describe what a healthy response would be.

In triads have the clergy explain why they rated themselves as they did and what steps they think might be taken to improve their ratings. Explain that by verbalizing their ratings, they will gain a greater understanding of the steps that need to be taken.

Suggest that they ask other members of the triad to hold each other accountable and perhaps even check in on each other between this and the next meeting. You might even have some fun by establishing a small reward for the person in the triad that makes the most progress.

TWENTY AREAS OF CONTRAST

1. High Education—Low Salary

   (Your Number _____)

   HC understand that they will not get rich in the ministry.

   UC resent the higher income of comparably educated people in other professions.

2. The Food We Eat

   (Your Number _____)

   HC are tempted by fast foods, sweet drinks, and other unhealthy diets but normally resist them.

   UC indulge in such foods in response to stress and emotional tiredness.

3. Time for Physical Exercise

   (Your Number _____)

   HC see regular physical exercise as part of the stewardship of their bodies.

   UC do not have time to exercise, given their demanding schedule.

4. Responding to Verbal Abuse

   (Your Number _____)

   HC look behind abusive behavior by others and see a wounded person.

   UC see such abusive behavior as a challenge to their personal dignity.

5. Questions and Doubts

(Your Number _____)

HC experience times of deep questioning and doubt.

UC are consumed by their questions and dominated by their doubts.

6. Responding to Criticism

(Your Number _____)

HC listen for pastoral opportunities in criticism but do not take the criticism personally.

UC see all criticism as an attack on their personhood.

7. The Value of Play

(Your Number _____)

HC have several different ways to have fun or unwind when there is time.

UC feel irresponsible when they take time to unwind.

8. Families Often Pay a Price

(Your Number _____)

HC struggle with the sacrifices that ministry makes on their families.

UC see family needs as a burden that interferes with their ministry.

9. Having Fun With the Family

(Your Number _____)

HC seek ways to have fun with their families in both small and big experiences.

UC do not know how to play with the family even when there is time.

10. God Has Called Me to Ministry

(Your Number _____)

HC recognize God's call includes challenges and even suffering.

UC keep seeking the perfect call where everything feels right.

11. Spirit of the Living God, Breathe on Me

(Your Number _____)

HC sense the Spirit's movement in the good and the bad.

UC feel despair is a sign of God's abandonment.

12. Personal Spiritual Practices

(Your Number _____)

HC make time for personal spiritual practices a priority.

UC neglect spiritual disciplines because there is not enough time.

13. To Whom Does Scripture Speak

(Your Number _____)

HC approaches Scripture with the question: "What is God saying to me?"

UC approach Scripture with the question: "How can I use this in a sermon?"

14. The Focus of Our Prayers

(Your Number _____)

HC pray for other people and for greater understanding in their ministry.

UC pray about being misunderstood and underappreciated.

15. Thinking About the Future

(Your Number _____)

HC take time to muse and play with possibilities for the future.

UC are too busy to play or imagine the future.

16. Faith and Success

(Your Number _____)

HC recognize that faithful ministry does not always appear successful.

UC are shaped by the world's definition of success.

17. The Success of Other Clergy

(Your Number _____)

HC celebrate God's work in other clergies' ministries.

UC are envious and critical of other clergies' ministries.

18. Sexual Attraction

(Your Number _____)

HC occasionally feel sexual attraction to others.

UC feel the same attraction but do not understand appropriate boundaries.

19. Being Anxious in Anxious Times

(Your Number _____)

HC trust in the sovereignty of God that eases their anxiety in difficult times.

UC allow difficulties to increase their anxiety and makes them critical of others.

20. Who Is the Savior?

(Your Number _____)

HC recognize that God's grace is made perfect in our weakness.

UC confuse salvation by personal effort with salvation by faith.

Create a graph that allows you to picture your movement from 1 to 100 in each of the 20 areas.

Your group may want to add other areas of contrast and include them in your continuum. You may also want to discuss whether you agree with the way a particular category is described. As you discuss them with each other, you may also find yourself adjusting your ratings. Have fun and enjoy yourself. It is not perfection but insight that you are seeking.

Don't forget that God's power is made perfect in our weakness and God's grace often is made visible in unexpected ways.

Inform the group that for meeting six the discussion will center around issues raised in the story "The Gift Not Received" in Volume 2, *Clergy Tales–Tails: Wagging, Friendly but Exhausting.* It can be found on Amazon at *amzn.to/1a1uCI6.* Ask them to read "The Gift Not Received" before they come. Establish both the time and location for the next meeting.

MEETING SIX

CLERGY ENVY

Each time you gather, allow ample time to check in with each other and to have the appropriate food and beverage. Always allow people to raise issues and questions that have occurred to them since the last meeting. You might also have some fun asking how people felt about the progress they have made on moving up their graph.

"THE GIFT NOT RECEIVED"

As you begin to discuss "The Gift Not Received," ask for any general reactions to the story. When appropriate, the following questions can be offered for further discussion.

Allen hears the Dickerson family say:

"What we are about to tell you has absolutely nothing to do with you. In fact, what makes this so hard is that Ellen and I have so much respect and admiration for you." Then the man proceeds to share what is convincing them to change church membership—"the fun service in which the pastor was just an amazing and rather hilarious speaker." They described how "their children were almost dancing in the aisles to the lively music of the band and absolutely fascinated by the images projected on the screens throughout the auditorium."

1. Picture yourself hearing such a conversation with a member of your congregation. How does it make you feel?

2. What are the parallels to the experience of grief at a time of loss?

3. What are the healthiest ways that pastors can process experiences of grief upon hearing such a message?

EXPERIENCING THE CAIN AND ABEL STORY

4. In what way does the Cain and Able story reflect the experience of clergy who work hard but see other pastors experiencing more success in building their ministries?

5. What are some normal feelings pastors can have with respect to the success of other churches?

Allen discovers a secret that could damage Pastor Henry Harp's successful ministry that has attracted several of Allen's own membership away from his church.

"Now he held in his hand the power to kill or at least seriously damage Henry's career. The Cain and Abel story would not leave his mind. He remembered God saying to Cain in response to his anger, 'Sin is lurking at the door; its desire is for you, but you must master it.'"

6. How would you describe the power of sins like envy, fear of failure, desire for success, and jealousy affecting the ministry of pastors?

7. What are resources that help pastors respond in a healthy manner to such feelings?

MEGACHURCHES AND TRADITIONAL WORSHIP

Allen reflects on what he considers the theory behind megachurch growth.

"He knew the whole theory of megachurch growth was to remove all the symbols from what he would call the sanctuary and they called the gathering area. Sermons made brief references to Scripture but mainly focused on uplifting lessons about life. Music was geared to be upbeat and shaped by the latest trends in the culture. The programs of the church combined entertainment and building supportive life skills together with some opportunities to engage in missions that made the participants feel good about what they were doing."

8. How fair do you think Allen's description of growth churches is?

9. How would you describe the theory behind such church growth?

10. What are their strengths and what are their weaknesses?

11. What are the strengths and weaknesses behind a more traditional approach to church ministry?

PASTORS REACHING OUT TO EACH OTHER

When Allen heard about Henry's battle with cancer, despite his previous thoughts, he immediately called him.

"'I just heard the news about your cancer and wanted to call and offer my prayers of support. I thought that perhaps it might be of help to talk to another pastor.' . . . At that moment, the barriers had been removed. They were two pastors reaching out to each other."

12. What makes it difficult to reach out to other pastors of a different theological stream?

13. What might be the impact if we deliberately chose to do that?

14. How willing would you be to experiment with reaching out to a pastor of a different theological persuasion without waiting for a crisis as an excuse?

15. Would you be willing to do that before the next meeting and report on your experience?

NEXT TIME

Remind the group that they have now completed six meetings. Tell them that there still are several short stories and a full-length mystery novel that they can discuss if they want to recommit to additional meetings.

If there are those who do not wish to continue, encourage them to secure colleague support in other ways, thank them for their participation, and have communal prayer for each other.

If there are sufficient numbers to continue, remind them that next time they will discuss "Did God Say?" *amzn.to/1a1uCI6.*

MEETING SEVEN

A Path to Clergy Addiction

This discussion is based on the second story in Volume 2, *Clergy Tales–Tails: Wagging, Friendly but Exhausting.* The story is "Did God Say?" *amzn.to/1a1uCI6.* Enjoy the story first before gathering to reflect on it with your colleagues.

Continue to allow ample time to check in, share some food, and raise any questions that have occurred since the last time. If there were those who dropped out, take some time to process the groups feelings about their missing members. You might even discuss whether there are other ways that members can continue to offer the missing members colleague support.

If your group is reduced in numbers and you want to consider adding some new members, recognize the challenge of how to integrate the new members into your group. Consider specific steps to take to make the group comfortable with each other.

As you begin to reflect on "Did God Say?" allow people to share their general reactions to the story. Because they are familiar with the process by now, they may raise issues about ministry that you have identified for further discussion. Simply acknowledge them and point out that you will be discussing them later. If they do raise additional issues, make sure that the group does return to these issues at some point in the discussion.

EXHAUSTED BY TEDIUM

Charles, the pastor in the story "Did God Say?", contrasts the thrill of being called by God and the exhausting tedium of the daily tasks in ministry.

"What a thrilling thought to be working for God. However, when your call results in being a pastor of a modest-size church in a small Midwestern city, the work can become rather tedious.

"I know the old joke about only having to work one hour a week, but the congregation seems more than willing to fill in the rest of the hours as well. Two or three nights a week, there is some committee meeting. During the day, there are hospital visits to make, Bible studies to conduct, planning for youth groups, community work with other pastors, and responding to the inevitable family crisis or request for personal counseling."

1. What are practices that other clergy have discovered that help a pastor keep in touch with the source of call and satisfactions in ministry and resist being worn down by the daily tedium of ministry?

FINANCIAL PRESSURE

As Charles reflects on the tensions of not being able to provide adequately for his family, he thinks:

"It made me feel like less of a man when I could not provide for my family. Marie would agree that neither of us dreamed of being rich. We just wanted not to have migraines each month as we tried to stretch my small paycheck to meet our many bills. Occasionally we wanted to afford some little extras."

2. To what degree do you think inadequate financial resources distract pastors from their satisfaction in ministry?

3. What other features of ministry sometimes challenge a pastor's self-image?

BEING ADDICTED TO THE THRILL

Charles reflects on the addictive quality of his own unethical behavior.

"I must admit there was also a little thrill to the clandestine nature of my efforts. . . . I have read news articles about politicians, financial wizards, lawyers, and CEOs of large corporations getting caught accepting bribes or engaging in creative and profitable money-making schemes. These were not people who were living in poverty. I often wondered what made them risk everything to get a little bit more when they already had enough.

"I think I understand now. It was not about the money. It was the thrill of living on the edge. It was sort of like an addiction. It began with some small rationalization that justified my actions. Then there was a thrill of getting away with it. It made me feel smarter than others. Then, like dope, the old thrill was not enough. You had to raise the stakes, take more risks, and prove to yourself how brilliant you really were."

4. Do you think it is possible that sometimes clergy also take risky behavior, even unethical behavior, because it adds some thrill to what has become a boring, even if exhausting, life?

5. Most addictive behavior involves some form of denial of the power that the behavior has over the person. How would you describe Charles' form of denial?

6. What scenario can you imagine that might break through his denial? In essence you are imagining an alternative ending to the story.

7. How do you respond to his analysis of such behavior becoming addictive?

YOU WILL BE LIKE GOD

Charles reflects on how the isolation caused by his secret behavior is similar to what happened to Adam and Eve in the garden.

"While you yearned to tell someone else so that they could admire how clever you were, you could not really do that. So you became a god, creating your own little universe, and setting your own standards of right and wrong. (You have eaten the fruit of the knowledge of good and evil.)"

8. Are there other ways that ministry tempts one to "become a god unto oneself?" How do you avoid such a pitfall?

9. As a group, build a list of 5–10 addictive behaviors that clergy can find tempting?

10. What role do you think a combination of mind-numbing demands and feelings of being underappreciated play in a person's susceptibility to such temptations?

Tell them that they will be reading "The Tempting Fruit" for the next meeting, Volume 2, *Clergy Tales–Tails: Wagging, Friendly but Exhausting* available at *amzn.to/1a1uCI6*.

MEETING EIGHT

PREJUDICE AND A CONGREGATION'S COMFORT

Once they have checked in, shared food, and are ready for group conversation, you can begin.

You are now well into the process. You might take some time for the group to discuss the impact of *A Company of Pastors* on their ministry.

Then turn to "The Tempting Fruit," in Volume 2, *Clergy Tales–Tails: Wagging, Friendly but Exhausting.*

Ask for general reactions and comments.

CHANGE IS UNCOMFORTABLE

While this story is set in 1984 and women clergy are more widely accepted now, there are still many ways in which churches demonstrate society's prejudices in their response to different types of clergy.

1. How would you describe the ideal image of a clergy person that most churches want?

2. Speak about the pressure you have felt in being compared to this ideal image.

3. What are some of the prejudices that you recognize still exist that affect a church's acceptance of a pastor?

Beth felt that one of the ways prejudice was expressed was by people being hypercritical of her performance as a clergy person. They wanted to find fault to justify their prejudice. Her friend, Shirley, responds by saying:

"Not surprised. Most of us have learned to adjust to life as it is. Threaten to change things, and it means that we all have to reevaluate who we are. Familiar pain is more comfortable than the unknown future."

4. To what degree to you agree or disagree with Shirley's evaluation of people's response to change? How does that affect your ministry?

NOT EVERYONE LIKES A SERMON

After one of Beth's sermons, she gets this response:

"As a longtime member, he wanted to remind her that this congregation was made up of good people who needed to be praised for their good works and not told that they had failed to reach out to a lot of likely undeserving vagrants and illegal immigrants. The very idea of suggesting that our dear Lord and Savior might have been an illegal immigrant when his family fled to Egypt was just insulting."

5. How should clergy balance their affirmation of people and the challenge of the Gospel to alter people's lives?

6. Name five unhealthy responses that clergy can make to being criticized.

7. How should clergy respond to people's criticism when a sermon has offended?

A GRACEFUL INTERRUPTION

In a time of tension, Beth visits a young couple and their newly born twins in the hospital, the following takes place:

"The couple burst into wide grins when they saw Beth enter their room. 'Come see what we have,' they cried. Beth had the pleasure of saying the first prayer to welcome two healthy children into the world.

"'You get part of the credit,' Tommy said.

"'Tommy's right,' Lila agreed. 'Without your support and counseling, I'm not sure we would have gotten this far. The boy will be Thomas, Jr., but we've decided to name the girl Elizabeth after you.'

"For once Beth was speechless, but the tears flowing down her cheeks were message enough for the Fletchers."

8. How often have you experienced an interruption to difficult moments in your ministry by some event that reminds you of the blessing of being a pastor?

GOD'S CURRICULUM

9. How accurate is Beth's statement?

"The temptation you face [in leaving] seminary [is you] think you have all this knowledge about what is right and wrong for the church. You come to a congregation and discover that only God knows the truth about good and evil. What you have to do is care about the people and trust God."

10. Share some things that God has taught you through the members of your congregation.

YOUR BEST ADVICE

11. What are five statements of wisdom the group would offer a pastor who has just left seminary and is beginning service at a church?

Tell the group that for the next meeting you are going to discuss some of the thoughts that the author offered in the "Why I write these tales" section of volume 2 of *Clergy Tales—Tails amzn.to/1a1uCI6.*

MEETING NINE

IMPERFECT CHURCHES WITH IMPERFECT PASTORS

Once everyone has arrived and shared thoughts and experiences that have occurred since the last meeting, you will then guide them into the author's reflections on ministry and the nature of the church.

ACCEPTANCE OF THE UNQUALIFIED

1. How do members respond to the statement of theologian Shirley Guthrie?

"The church is the only 'club' in the world that accepts as members only those who are not qualified to belong to it!" (*Christian Doctrine*, page 357)

2. If you accept that statement, name two or three ways that it affects your ministry?

3. As you reflect together on what is happening in our churches today, how do you respond to the statement:

"God is neither dependent on our purity nor defeated by the acts of faithlessness of clergy or congregation. Ministry is a complex mosaic of strengths and weaknesses in a confusing and sin-filled world."

4. Identify three examples from Scripture where God chose to work through imperfect people or groups.

5. Why do you think God chooses to work through imperfect people, churches, and clergy?

THE MIRACLE OF THE CHURCH

6. In light of your own experience, how do you react to the author's statement:

"Ministers are strong and weak, faithful and faithless, as are the members of their congregations. Yet each week clergy gather with their congregations to hear the Scriptures, sing the songs, and pray the prayers that remind them that there is more to life than meets the eye. When we are honest in our confession of sins, we discover that our hope rests in a power beyond ourselves, and there is reason for hope. The miracle of the church is not in our faithfulness but in God's faithfulness. We are witnesses to how our confused reality keeps being interrupted by grace."

7. If your congregation accepted that statement as true, how do you think it would affect their support of your ministry?

8. What are ways that you might engage your congregation in reflecting on that statement?

STANDING IN THE BREACH

9. When you reflect on your own call to ministry, how is the author's statement an accurate description of your vocation:

"Clergy stand in the breach between God and humanity. We, too, are imperfect, but we have been called by God. Like Moses in leading the people of Israel out of Egypt, we find ourselves speaking to the people on behalf of God and also turning to beg for God's mercy on behalf of the people. We often feel like neither audience is listening, but we are not free to abandon our call."

BEING INTENTIONAL ABOUT HEALTH

The Duke Clergy Health Initiative documents the dramatic decline in the health of clergy in recent years. For example, the study found 79% of clergy had weight problems that led to diabetes, heart problems, blood pressure, etc. They also discovered the depression rate among clergy was twice the national average.

10. As a group, consider some of the reasons why clergy health is declining in such a dramatic way.

11. As individuals, respond to two questions:

    What are two ways that you are being conscious of the need to pay attention to the maintenance of your own health?

    What is one new way that you would like to begin?

A PASTOR'S FAMILY

12. Think about the impact that your being a pastor has on your family.

    What positive impact on your family do you hope for?

    What negative impact concerns you in their being part of a pastor's family?

13. How do you respond to the idea of playing the family

game offered in this volume of *Clergy Tales—Tails amzn. to/1a1uCI6* with your family?

Would you consider joining another clergy family and playing it together?

At the next meeting, the focus of the discussion will be the story "Truth Has Consequences" in Volume 3, *Clergy Tales–Tails: When God Wags the Tale amzn.to/15TORlR.*

MEETING TEN

TRUTH HAS CONSEQUENCES

The focus of this meeting will be the issues for ministry raised by the story "Truth Has Consequences" in Volume 3, *Clergy Tales—Tails: When God Wags the Tale, amzn.to/15TORlR.*

PROTECTING CLERGY PRIVACY

For the sake of discussion, let us use the name of Paul for the pastor in the story.

Paul makes the following statement about clergy availability:

"Clergy are always caught in the bind of wanting to be accessible but also needing periods of uninterrupted time to accomplish a myriad of other tasks. Some use their secretary or an irritating electronic voice offering a variety of button options in order to protect their privacy. Having experienced the frustration of trying to get past such barriers myself, and perhaps not wanting the church's message to be one of unavailability, I chose to keep my office door open to all visitors."

1. What are the pros and cons of such openness?

2. What is the best way to balance being open to people's needs and maintaining a measure of privacy in order to concentrate on other tasks?

SERMONS PREACHED AND SERMONS HEARD

Sometimes when you proclaim the truth it has unintended consequences. A pastor is responsible for what s/he preaches but has little control over what people hear.

Paul makes some comments about interacting with others regarding a sermon he has preached:

"I confess, as I've heard many preachers admit, that once a sermon is preached, I quickly put it out of my mind as I begin to focus on what is next. Besides, I hadn't preached for too many years before I realized that what people hear can be at wide variance with what I thought I had said. When someone wants to comment on a past sermon, particularly one preached several weeks in the past, I often make some vague response in hopes that what they say next will jog my memory, and I won't appear to be a complete dolt."

3. What is your experience with respect to people wanting to discuss a sermon you have preached?

4. How does it affect your preaching to know that people can hear something totally different from what you intended to communicate in a sermon?

5. How can we assist the congregation in recognizing that in addition to our responsibility to preach well, they have a responsibility to listen well?

ON NOT BEING DEFENSIVE

Paul heard Eleanor tell him what she had heard and how it had affected her family. Later as Paul reflected on the experience, he thought:

"I remember feeling very frightened that I might say the wrong thing. I knew for certain that I had to avoid getting defensive about what she had heard in the sermon. This was not about me but about her."

At the time, Paul responded:

"Eleanor, I can't take back the sermon, but I can help you think this through if you are willing to talk about it some more."

6. How does one avoid becoming defensive when a sermon had a serious impact on another person?

    Let us consider the particular incident of sexuality that Eleanor brought to Paul.

7. What is your approach as a pastor when you are confronted with any shocking incidents in the life of a person who comes to you?

8. How does it affect your approach to recognize that when a person seeks counsel of a pastor, they are looking for spiritual answers as well as practical advice?

9. What are some ways that a pastor conveys the healing grace of God to people caught in complex, even devastating, circumstances?

REFRAMING

Eleanor reports that she thought that her husband's secret was that he was having an affair.

"I'm now convinced I know what is coming, and I am angry. 'Who is she?' I asked.

"Then came the bomb shell. He looked up at me and with more pain than I think I have ever seen in a person's eyes. He said, 'That's the problem. It isn't another woman.' Then, in almost a whisper, he said, 'It's a man.'"

> 10. Even though you have already read the story, try to step outside of how Paul responded and consider what you think your first response would have been and why?

Eleanor reports that this whole revelation occurred in response to a sermon that Paul had preached on truth-telling. She then shares her Christian understanding about homosexuality based on both childhood memories and infrequent sermons that she has heard in the media.

> 11. How often does a person's inadequate theology become the first challenge for the pastor who is seeking to help?

Paul responds by saying:

"Let's separate things out a bit. At this moment, are you angriest at me for the sermon, the Bible, or your husband?"

> 12. What was Paul trying to do with such a question?

> 13. When is it important for a pastor to help a distraught person to step back from their immediate pain and view it from a larger perspective?

14. What is your reaction to Paul's attempt to reframe the question by saying:

"Jesus never said anything about homosexuality, but he did speak about the almost sacred quality of the covenant of marriage. That's the real sin we are dealing with. . . .The real question that we need to deal with is that the covenant of your marriage has been broken. What would you have done differently if it had been another woman?"

UNDERSTANDING BOUNDARIES

15. How do you understand what happened when Eleanor began to flaunt her sexuality before Paul?

16. In recent years, there have been many suggestions about how a pastor should guard against such situations—leaving the office door open, always having a witness present, etc. What is lost and what is gained by how pastors choose to protect themselves by such actions?

17. While it becomes clear that Paul has a particular theological position with respect to homosexuality and the church, how did he, how does any pastor, stay true to his or her understanding but also respond in a healing way to a person's distress?

Remind the group that at the next meeting the focus will be on the story "A Hypocritical Oath for Pastors" *amzn.to/15TORlR in* Volume 3, *When God Wags the Tale.*

MEETING ELEVEN

A HYPOCRITICAL
OATH FOR PASTORS

A MINISTRY OF PRESENCE

While visiting the seminary campus, Mark's quiet day is interrupted by a bullet that shatters the window as he leaves the campus bookstore. He spots the shooter in the bell tower. On impulse, Mark runs to the tower and climbs to the roof where he encounters Ethan, a pastor whom Mark had taught in seminary.

"Ethan swung his rifle around to face Mark. 'What are you doing here, professor?'

"'I thought I was coming to the campus for a break from church work, but your rather dramatic statement caught my attention, so I thought I'd come up and see what you were trying to say.' He remembered from watching TV that you were supposed to establish a relationship with the shooter. 'By the way, you can call me Mark.' He edged towards Ethan as he spoke. He didn't know what he was going to do, but that was the way he remembered it from the movies."

1. You may not have encountered a sniper in your ministry, but there are probably several parallel, if less dramatic, encounters where you had no choice but to respond. What are the resources that you draw upon at such times?

2. Mark's decision reflects what is often called the "ministry of presence." What is your understanding of what that means in the exercise of your ministry?

THE SINS OF THE CHURCH

In the story, Ethan is a clergyman who has lost his faith. He expresses that in dialogue with Mark.

"'How long have you been a minister, Mark, twenty years?'

"'Close to twenty-five now,' Mark said.

"'How'd you do it?' Mark could hear the stress in his voice. 'Didn't you ever realize that resurrection is biologically impossible, forgiveness is for wimps who can't win, and all the church is interested in is sucking the money out of gullible members to protect a failing institution?'

Ethan continues his indictment of the church. "We work for a church that is collapsing from within because it is so self-serving and full of hypocrisy that no one under thirty will darken its doors. . . . Even the older generation is beginning to abandon it because their beach house offers more comfort on the weekend. They would rather spend their money on pleasure than on sharing with those in need as the Gospel commands."

Many pastors have entertained similar doubts themselves. Mark recognizes that in himself. *The irony is, I share some of his anger only I've learned to survive. Maybe I'm the crazy one.*

3. What are the factors that allow some clergy to continue despite the doubts and the church failures they see while others conclude that they need to leave the ministry?

THE INTEGRITY OF MINISTRY

4. You can probably add to Ethan's list of indictments of the church. What are some of your strategies for coping with the disconnect between Christian behavior and what you believe the church is called to be in Scripture?

In the story, Ethan challenges the very integrity of ministry.

"'Face it, Mark. Don't you feel like a hypocrite, getting up Sunday after Sunday and telling people that they should love a neighbor who is willing to betray them to make a few more dollars? I'll bet you tell them that they should trust your absentee God—a god who is willing to allow untold innocent children to starve in this world while Christians support governments who waste billions of dollars building weapons to destroy each other.'

"'Isn't God supposed to be all knowing? Didn't the Almighty One know from the beginning that he was creating a universe in which such cruelty would continue to exist? A child with tinker toys could make a better creation than that.'"

5. Do you believe that God knew what God was doing when God created the universe and first called Israel and later established the church to minister to the world?

6. How do you explain to others the disconnect between church behavior and God's call to the church?

THE HYPOCRITICAL OATH OF CLERGY

7. How do you feel about Mark's response when he says:

"You asked me a question, Ethan. The answer is I do feel like a hypocrite, sometimes."

"I think it is one of the unspoken burdens of the ministry. We are not given the luxury of taking a few months off when we are filled with doubts. Rather, we have to stand up each Sunday morning and try to offer hope and courage to a people who are desperate for some good news that will help them survive."

8. Do you agree that this is a burden of ministry for many clergy?

Mark puts a positive spin on the definition of hypocrite.

"Life gets overwhelming at times. All good pastors are hypocrites. When life gets rough and the questions are without answers, they playact as if it is true until people can believe again. That's what it means to be a hypocrite—to playact at the truth."

9. Should pastors only speak of what they know to be true or is it OK to sometimes proclaim what they want to be true?

WHAT WILL THEY REMEMBER?

In the final scene in the hospital, Ethan speaks of how Mark's behavior impacted him.

"I'll still have my doubts, but you reflected the God I want to believe in. If I had fallen, my life would have ended without value. I was totally focused on myself. If you had fallen to your death, your life would still have had value, not only to me but to those who witnessed what you did and to those who told the story to others."

10. How do you evaluate Ethan's analysis of Mark's ministry to him?

11. What does that say about authority in ministry?

12. How do you react to the idea that ministers take a hypocritic oath as pastors?

Remind the group that for meeting thirteen, you will be discussing the third story, "A Grief Observed," in Volume 3 of *Clergy Tales—Tails: When God Wags the Tale, amzn.to/15TORlR.*

MEETING TWELVE

BENEATH THE PUBLIC IMAGE

WHEN CLERGY TURN ON THEMSELVES

This third story in *Clergy Tales—Tails: When God Wags the Tale amzn. to/15TORlR* begins with the pastor, Allen, returning home after an exhausting and frustrating day. It has clearly assaulted Allen's sense of self-worth. Distracted by his thoughts, he turns his car too sharply and hits the curb as he enters his driveway. It makes Allen feel stupid. In a negative frame of mind, he castigates himself, "Way to go, Allen, you dumb shit. Lucky that none of your neighbors are out for an evening stroll."

1. What causes pastors to turn on themselves when they have had a series of negative experiences?

2. In what way is Allen trying to expunge himself of his anger by using such language on himself?

3. How does this parallel with Psalm 22:6ff, "But I am a worm, and not human; scorned by others and despised by the people."?

4. What other strategies do pastors use at such times?

PASTORS AND CRUDE LANGUAGE

While most pastors have learned to discipline themselves and avoid crude language in public utterances, sometimes, in private, that discipline crumbles. When Allen's wife, Marcia, tries to empathize with her frustrated husband, he explodes:

"'It was a perfect day. I consider it one of the privileges of my life to feed the egos of a bunch of self-indulgent prima donnas. Those fucking morons couldn't distinguish an ethical value from a Krispy Kreme donut.'"

5. Do you think it is hypocritical or understandable that occasionally in private clergy will use crude language and exaggerated characterization about their experiences?

6. How do you relate this to some of the strong language of the Psalms?

GRIEF FOR PROFESSIONALS

When Marcia invites a psychologist friend, Phyllis, to meet with Allan and her, Phyllis shares an experience she had in a hospital that alerted her to the problem of grief for medical personnel.

"One day over at the hospital, I opened a wrong door by accident and found one of the hospital's best surgeons weeping in the closet. He had just lost a little girl in surgery. Like the compassionate person he was, he had sat with the family for over an hour absorbing their pain. Then he left them with the chaplain. No one noticed him entering the closet.

"'I guess people are so focused on the family of the person who has died that they never think about the impact on the medical staff,' I say."

7. What is your understanding of the effect on a person of
    not attending to their grief and keeping it locked up inside?

8. How does this apply to the experience of pastors?

HOW GRIEF AFFECTS US

In addition to naming the stages of grief–denial, anger, bargaining, and
acceptance–Allen speaks of the effects of grief on the person:

"'Physically it makes the person's body more vulnerable to breakdown,
and they lack energy,' I say.

"'And emotionally,' she presses.

"'I'm not sure what the studies show,' I say, 'but from my experience,
people in grief become more isolated. They lose perspective, as well as
emotional control. Their pain is so great that they are almost entirely
self-absorbed.'"

9. Would you add anything to Allen's assessment?

A PASTOR'S GRIEF

Phyllis suggests that the same effects of grief in a parishioner's life may
apply to a clergy's grief when it is not resolved.

10. Quickly as a group, name five to ten circumstances in the
    ministry that may cause a pastor to experience personal grief.

HELPING OTHERS WITH THEIR GRIEF

11. How do you evaluate Allen's description of how a pastor helps individuals and a congregation deal with their grief?

"Mostly [I] just listened. When people are in deep grief, they feel like their lives are in chaos. All the familiar structures that used to give them a sense of security have vanished. You understand this. Mostly you encourage them to tell stories, including hopefully some fun ones, to remind them of the good memories that they share. Words help us give form to our feelings and bring some order to our chaos."

12. Are there other strategies that you would add to his list?

CONGREGATIONS FEEL GRIEF TOO

Phyllis asks about how Allen attends to the congregation's feelings of grief.

"Congregations always feel helpless at such times. Deep pain scares all of us, yet most people don't know how to respond. Sometimes they even try to explain why the tragedy happened, which isn't helpful to the family at all."

He then proceeds to explain how he urges the members to take simple actions like preparing food, writing notes, offering to help out in simple tasks. His suggestion is that this helps the members regain some control over the feelings of helplessness they experience in the face of tragedy.

13. Are there additional ways you help a congregation respond to grief?

PAYING ATTENTION TO YOUR OWN GRIEF

When Phyllis presses Allen about how he attended to his own feelings of grief, he responds:

"There wasn't time to pay attention to my needs. In addition to the funeral and being present to them, I had a Sunday service coming up, a budget meeting to prepare for, two baptisms, and a newsletter to get out. I think I also had to speak to the custodian about some member's complaint about cleaning."

14. How often do you find yourself in a similar situation where the demands of ministry don't offer you the luxury of pausing to attend to your personal feelings?

15. What is the effect on pastors who continue to move past their personal pain because they want to respond to the needs of others?

16. Does this relate to the Duke study that found depression rate among pastors was 8.7 percent, which is higher than the national average of 5.5? Another study found clergy depression at 11.1% or more than double the national average.

17. How do you respond to the tension between legitimate demands of ministry and paying attention to your own personal needs of self-care?

CUMULATIVE GRIEF

Phyllis presses:

"I've talked enough with Marcia to know that there are many areas of grief that you experience in the ministry. What I want to suggest to you is that they are cumulative."

"I understand what you are saying, but what you don't understand is that's just the way it is in the ministry," I say.

"I don't doubt that," says Phyllis. "The question is how does a good pastor handle his or her grief without getting locked into denial and, like many doctors, building shields around themselves for protection."

18. Building on your own understanding of the effects of unresolved grief on individuals, identify some ways that pastors might act out their unresolved grief inappropriately.

19. Try to formulate three or four strategies for how pastors can take their grief seriously and avoid being locked into denial.

Tell the group that in the next meeting, they will discuss some of the issues raised in the author's afterword about the nature of ministry. They can find it in Volume 3 of *Clergy Tales—Tails: When God Wags the Tale amzn.to/15TORlR.*

MEETING THIRTEEN

YOU (INSERT YOUR NAME)
ARE CALLED BY GOD

POSITIVE AND NEGATIVE STRESS

The author of *Clergy Tales—Tails* speaks of the nature of ministry.

"When one seeks to understand the nature of ministry, it is important to recognize that not all stress comes from negative experiences. The ministry is filled with very positive and affirming interactions that cause a pastor to feel awed that s/he is privileged to be a part of them. Yet, even these types of experiences place a drain on one's emotional reserves.

"High octane experiences, both negative and positive, frequently tumble on top of each other in the ministry. They are interspersed with many mundane, even tedious, demands of the profession that take their toll in a different form. There is a particular danger of moving from an adrenaline-pumping event in one moment to a mind-numbing meeting that solves nothing the next moment. Mix that with listening to how someone has taken offense at something you did, or the heart-breaking experience of watching a friend's marriage disintegrate, or the pain of strangers who have come to you in desperate need for help and you have a sense of the daily encounters in the ministry. Many clergy fail to recognize the critical need to return to the well frequently for refreshment."

1. Is this an accurate description of ministry as you experience it?

2. How would you speak of the critical need to return to the well for refreshment?

3. What are the ways that you have found to return to that well?

HOW IS YOUR BALANCE?

4. On a scale of 1, paying total attention to self and your personal needs, to 10, paying total attention to the needs of the congregation, where would you place yourself?

5. What are some of your behaviors that reflect how you live out that balance?

YOU HAVE BEEN CHOSEN BY GOD

6. How do you feel when you consider the statement, "You have been chosen by God," as applying to you?

   Let each person make a one or two sentence statement of what it means to be "Called by God."

Consider the author's statement:

"In the last several decades, the sense of call has been downplayed because it seemed to many that we were claiming to be somehow better than others. In many ways, we struggle with the assumption of arrogance attributed to Israel that they countered by saying that it was not that Israel was better, but the miracle was that God took a no people and made them God's people and that reflects the awe of our calling (1 Peter 2:10). It is not because of any quality in our lives but

because of the mysterious choice of God that we have been touched
for this special calling.

"Even at its most boring, there is something special about the ministry,
and frequently it is a full-time, hair-raising adventure that is anything
but boring. Yet critical to a healthy participation in that adventure is
our ability to return to the well often and be refreshed by the Spirit."

    7.   How do you react to that statement?

REVIVING OUR SENSE OF CALL

The author states:

"To be called by God for the pastoral ministry (and there are many
other calls to which God can call us) is to be spoken to by a voice from
beyond time and space to serve a people who also are called by God for
a particular ministry in our world. Yet with all of the facets of ministry,
it is easy to be overwhelmed by the demands of the profession and lose
touch with the source of our call. The necessary mundane nature of
many of the demands of ministry can also blur the special nature of
this body, the Body of Christ, chosen to incarnate God's expression
of truth."

    8.   Consider as a group how important it is to intentionally
        engage in reconnecting with your sense of call.

As a group, share the litany "God's Been There, Done That."

God's Been There Done That

God, I can't afford to give up the security of my profession to answer your call unless you can be more specific about what's ahead.

That's what Abram said when I called him and Sarai to leave their country, kindred, father's house and land.

Genesis 12:1

God, I'm too young, and I lack the courage to be a good pastor.

That's what Jeremiah said when I wanted him to call the nation to repentance. "I'm only a boy and I am afraid."

Paraphrased Jeremiah 1:7-*8*

God, I'm not a good speaker and pastors have to be eloquent.

That's what Moses said when I asked him to go and persuade Pharaoh. "I have never been eloquent . . . I am slow of speech and slow of tongue."

Exodus 4:10

God, I'm not a leader and could never get enough people to follow me to be effective.

That's what Gideon said, and I told him that if he had a large army and defeated the enemy, they would brag about how good they were and never give me credit. I like working through people who everyone says aren't capable.

Judges 7:2

God, I'm not a good enough person to be a pastor.
Pastors should be people beyond reproach.

**That's what Isaiah said when I called him but I had
an angel touch him and said "your guilt has departed
and your sin is blotted out."**

Isaiah 6:7

God, you must be in error. I rejected the church a long
time ago.

**That's what Saul said when I met him on the road
to Damascus.**

Acts 9:1 ff

God, maybe you don't understand how the world works.
You have to have a position of power and wealth if you
are going to make a difference.

**You mean Jesus was in error when he said to his
disciples, "I'm sending you out like lambs into the
midst of wolves. Carry no purse, no bag, no sandals,
and greet no one on the road."?**

Luke 10:3-4

God, I don't have the wisdom to debate all those skeptics
out there. What would I say to convince them of the
truth?

**So let me get this straight, you don't know the
future, consider yourself too young, lack courage,
get tongue-tied when you speak, don't know how
to lead others, lack high moral qualities, and have
been a visible opponent of my church. Sounds like
the type of person I can work with.**

I'm giving you just one piece of advice. "Just as I have loved you, you also should love one another. By this everyone will know that you are my disciples, if you have love for one another."

John 13:34-35

9. How does such a litany affect your understanding of God's call in your personal life?

Remind the group that at the next meeting, you will discuss the "12 Steps to Spiritual Revitalization" described in the next chapter. Share the outline with them, and point out that this will require more time than their normal time frame. Ask whether they would like to experience this as a daylong retreat or schedule a couple of meetings within a week of each other. Make arrangements based on their decision.

MEETING FOURTEEN

TWELVE STEPS TO SPIRITUAL REVITALIZATION

This is a group exercise adapted from the personal retreat experience described at the end of Volume 3, of *Clergy Tales—Tails: When God Wags the Tale.*

This would be most effective if the group decided to take at least a day retreat together. Otherwise it may be experienced over a couple of meetings, but they should be more closely spaced than the previous meetings to maintain continuity.

If your group is larger than six or seven, for the sake of time, it will be best to form small groups of three to five people. With the exception of step one where you form the groups and step twelve where you reconvene, instructions for each step need to be provided for each group so that they can move through the steps at their own pace.

The total group should agree on a time schedule so that they can reconvene as a plenary group at an agreed upon time.

Twelve Steps to Spiritual Revitalization

(Revised for group participation)

Step One

Create several small groups of three or four persons for this experience.

Make sure each person has a pad of paper, Bible, laptop or notebook with Internet connection.

Step Two

Have some coffee or cold drinks and some snack food if you desire.

Let each person briefly share what they would hope for in experiencing some personal spiritual renewal.

Step Three

Let all members of the group take five or ten minutes in silence to deliberately note and release their thoughts about the pressures and demands of their lives and simply rest in the presence of God.

Let each page through the Psalms and identify three or four phrases that praise God. Have them reflect on what the chosen phrases say about the nature of God and then select the one that seems to stand out.

Invite the members to share their chosen phrase and what it means to them with the group.

Join in a time of "sentence prayer" with each person making use of another person's phrase of praise for God.

Remind the group that this is the God who has called them to ministry.

Step Four

Encourage everyone to stand, stretch, breathe, and then resume their seats.

Taking a pad of paper, let each person identify eight significant chapters in their lives and give those chapters titles.

In each chapter of their lives, everyone should identify the major factors: people, places, and challenges that moved them in one direction or another.

It might be something someone said, a course of study, a place visited on vacation, a good or bad experience. Not all of them will seem religious. They should not be overly descriptive but note the various turning points in their journey.

If some are married and others single, they should note that and how it affected their journey.

Encourage them to take time and do lots of musing and reflecting on their life in the process.

Step Five

Each person can then share with the group some of the most significant events.

If, as people talk, new thoughts occur, they should make note of those as well.

Step Six

Assume, for the purpose of this experience, that God had a hand in the previously noted twists and turns in the journey. Ask group members to review the list each has made and look for possible patterns in how God is working in their lives.

State that whether they are used to thinking of God's involvement in their lives in this manner or not, there is value in looking through this lens.

Step Seven

Talk among yourselves about churches near or far that offer interesting, challenging ministries. Also talk about non-parish-based ministries, even in other denominations, that offer opportunities that could be satisfying.

Discuss the ways in which such ministries might satisfy some aspect of the original sense of call for each of them.

Moving may be the furthermost thing from participants' minds at this time, but exploring the alternatives has the value of offering a backdrop for reflecting on their current positions.

Step Eight

Invite all of them to list, in no particular order, some of the biggest challenges of their present positions—both the positive and negative ones.

Ask them to meditate on those issues. If God has called them to this place and is present with them in ministry, what might God be saying to them about how they face some of these tests?

Step Nine

Take a short break, maybe a brief walk.

Then ask the group to talk among themselves about their present positions.

They should describe some of the most satisfying moments in their current ministry, either accomplishments or challenges that they have confronted.

Encourage them to look for ways that can increase the opportunity for more satisfying moments.

Each should identify some specific actions that s/he can take.

Step Ten

Ask participants to note the clues from the turning points in their past and the nature of the experiences that give them a sense of satisfaction.

Each person should write a short paragraph about the next five years of that person's life.

What would s/he like to see happen in that time?

As the paragraphs are shared with the group, invite people to share their responses.

Step Eleven

Having completed these steps, invite everyone to take at least fifteen minutes offering his or her thoughts and possibilities to God in silent prayer.

Step Twelve

Come together as a total group and allow people to share spontaneously a sentence or two about what they most celebrate and thank God for in being called to the ministry.

Inform the group that at their next meeting they will be invited to participate in several meetings around the mystery novel *A Star and a Tear* available in both print and electronic form on *Amazon amzn. to/1aTDdgs*.

MEETING FIFTEEN

REFLECTIONS ON A
STAR AND A TEAR

MYSTERIES IN LIFE AND MINISTRY

After gathering, securing some food and a drink, and catching up with each other, the leader will focus the group. Continue your practice of opening with prayer or whatever devotional act has become appropriate for the group.

Everyone should have secured a copy of *A Star and A Tear*. In this guide, the author refers to both chapter numbers and page numbers in the printed version of the book. Those who have a Kindle version will be able to search for the chapter and phrases being commented upon.

Since most people who become interested in reading a mystery will not want to delay completing the mystery over several months, mention that the discussion will focus on issues about the ministry stimulated by the book but does not require that you refrain from completing the story at your own pace. It might be helpful if members were clear in the early discussions as to whether they had completed the novel or whether it would be good to avoid any discussion that would spoil the ending for some.

Also, some of the issues raised will be similar to issues previously raised by earlier stories, and the group will determine whether upon reflection the subject invites revisiting the discussion for a fresh angle. If not, the discussion can be brief and then continue on to the next subject.

The division of the meetings around the novel is somewhat arbitrary. The leader needs to be guided by the depth of discussion around particular questions and the energy of the group. To push through all the questions in one session might risk avoiding some significant exchanges. Probably about an hour of discussion is sufficient. Then the next question can be picked up at the next meeting.

THE SIGNIFICANCE OF THE INSIGNIFICANT

As the novel begins, Frank looks back on what at the time had seemed a small event but turned out to have tragic results. In Chapter 1, page 1, Frank reflects,

"It's strange how a small seemingly insignificant incident can rip open your personal universe and alter your life forever."

He then proceeds to speak of the small event that cost his wife her life.

1. Can you think of parallel examples in either your life or someone else's life?

2. How does this fit into your theology?

THE EROSION OF TRUST IN THE CHURCH

In Chapter 2, page 20, Bob Godwin speaks of the impact of church scandals on the ministry. "Any scandal connected with religion served to confirm society's cynicism, and that made his work more difficult."

Later in Chapter 20, page 243, Frank says, "It used to be that both believer and nonbeliever readily entrusted the valued members of their family to a pastor, even in the most private of situation. . . . A lot of that culture of trust has eroded."

And he raises the question: "How do you minister authentically in an age of suspicion?"

3. As a group identify some of ways that church scandals, sexual or otherwise, have affected the trust relationship between pastor and congregation.

4. What are some strategies that can help overcome that challenge?

A TRICKY COMBINATION

In Chapter 4, page 58 (the incident with the widow Felicity Marshall), the story suggests that a combination of exhaustion, the inherent loneliness of ministry, and the genuine desire to be empathetic and helpful can be a dangerous combination for the pastor.

5. Does this suggest that really good pastors, who work hard and want to be empathetic to others, may be the most vulnerable?

6. Does the danger of inappropriate behavior cause some pastors to become too cautious and shield themselves from genuine interaction with people who are hurting?

In Chapter 5, page 62, we read, "Thinking of Reggie reminded Frank of the lepers in the Bible. As a sex offender, Reggie was marked as untouchable. He didn't have to ring a bell to warn people not to come near, but he registered his name as a sex offender on a public Web site."

7. Is the comparison apt?

8. Would you ever make such a comparison in a sermon? What type of reaction might you receive?

MEETING SIXTEEN

After appropriate food, fun and fellowship, the leader continues to guide the discussion.

A SEARCH FOR TRANCENDENCE

In Chapter 5, after a particularly difficult experience in his first pastorate, Frank decides to focus his thoughts during a sabbatical on what he terms "the strange, symbiotic relationship between sexuality and spirituality."

1. In what ways do people use both sexuality and spirituality in a search for transcendence?

In Chapter 20, page 245, Frank comments, "Both powerful faith experiences and sexual release are acts grasping for ecstasy and transcendence. It's not exclusive to the pastorate, but our profession makes us vulnerable."

2. What type of discussion would be helpful to pastors in understanding this phenomenon more deeply?

3. Should lay people be brought into this conversation as well?

THE POWER OF GOSSIP

In Chapter 9, page 109, the radio broadcaster makes use of some gossip he has heard about Frank to attack his integrity. When Oscar is processing the experience with Frank, he comments on the power of gossip in the church. "Gossip is like mercury," said Oscar. "It's bright

and attractive to the eye, but every time you try to gather it up, it slips away and finds a new location in which to shine."

4. As you are aware, Paul in Romans 1:29 equates gossip with such behavior as "envy, murder, strife, deceit, craftiness, . . ." etc. How seriously do you think members of your congregation view the sin of gossip?

5. What are strategies to counter the power of gossip in your congregation?

SERMON STYLES AND ARCHITECTURE

In chapter 10, pages 125-131, you are introduced to two styles of sermons.

6. How would you describe those styles?

7. What do you think are the strengths of each?

In Chapter 11, page 142, there is a physical description and implied commentary on the power of architecture to attract visitors. On page 205, there is an incident that raises the question of the power of church symbols. On page 226, there is commentary on the message of a chapel's architecture.

8. How would you design an ideal church in which the architecture conveys the message of the Gospel?

9. What are the dangers that some forms of architecture may have a negative effect on people?

10. What are some ways that you can make use of your current church's architecture to communicate aspects of the faith?

MEETING SEVENTEEN

MINISTRY IS BUILT ON RELATIONSHIPS

After appropriate fun, food, and fellowship, gather the group with prayer.

THE BELOVED COMMUNITY OF PASTORS

In Chapter 12, page 144, when the clergy of the city are gathered together to discuss the impact of the serial rapist on their ministry, Bob Godwin reflects on the pastors who had come to the meeting: "He knew that some of these pastors disliked each other intensely and were not interested in cooperating on anything. However, today events brought them together, . . ."

    1.   What are the main factors that cause pastors of the Christian faith to dislike or distrust each other?

Chapter 16, page 202, Frank says to Bob Godwin, "I think men of faith need to be in closer touch with each other. Maybe we could learn from each other. I believe another scandal of the church is our separation one from the other."

    2.   What would be the benefit of pastors of differing theological persuasions having more conversations with each other?

DANGER OF FANATICISM

In Chapter 13, page 160, Frank is speaking to the gathered clergy.

". . .we are certain of two things as we work with our congregations. First, none of us are pure, and we are cautious about those who are so eager to cast the first stone. Didn't you ever wonder what secrets those would-be-stone-throwers were hiding when Jesus asked the one without sin to cast the first stone?"

3. What is the danger of an over emphasis on purity in the church?

4. How do you strive for the good but avoid the danger of fanaticism?

SEXUAL ADDICTION

In exploring why some people get involved in inappropriate sexual behavior in Chapter 15, page 190, Frank comments,

"Sex becomes a reward for all the hard work he does, and maybe a salve for his wounds when things aren't going well."

Then he says,

". . . for some people, sex becomes like an addiction. But often it's not enough by itself. Each time, you have to enhance the experience with something more."

"'Like those politicians who use their position to seduce one of their followers but keep doing it in more dangerous circumstances until they get caught,' O'Riley said."

Then on page 286 Frank continues,

"You can be addicted to things other than drugs," Frank said, "but drugs give us the pattern to look at. Some people will experiment with drugs but then decide there are other things in life and just move on."

"[However] for some people, use doesn't decline," Frank continued. "Not only do they not give it up, but it escalates. The original pleasure is not enough. They want a stronger and stronger experience."

5. How does the image of addiction help in understanding some people's behavior with respect to sex?

MEETING EIGHTEEN

GOD'S PRIESTHOOD

Welcome everyone, check in, and catch up.

When all are settled, begin.

THE PRIESTHOOD OF ALL BELIEVERS

In Chapter 17, page 210, Wiley, the clerk of session at Frank's church, says,

"Hey, I just made sense out of one of the things you are always preaching about."

"What's that?"

"The priesthood of all believers," Wiley said. Wiley stood up and faced Frank with a stern look on his face. "Frank Sessions, you hopeless sinner, you are no better than the rest of us. Get on your knees, and let me pray that, in some unexplainable way, God can find it in his heart to forgive you." . . . Wiley reached down and grabbed his hands pulling him to his feet. Without explanation, he gave him a powerful bear hug, "Welcome to the God-blessed human race!"

1. What does the priesthood of all believers mean to you?

2. Recall a time when one of your members said or acted in a way that proclaimed the faith in a deep and enduring way.

A PASTOR'S FAMILY

In Chapter 19, page 224, and Chapter 20, page 237, there are comments regarding the impact of the ministry on the family of the pastor.

"The demands of a megachurch pastor—particularly the pressures of projecting images of success—may have contributed to tensions within the Godwin family."

"Frank could tell it had been hard on David living in the fishbowl of a pastor's family, exacerbated by the high-profile nature of Bob's ministry."

3. Discuss the impact on your own family and those of other pastor colleagues in being part of a pastor's family.

4. Identify both some of the benefits and the challenges.

MEETING NINETEEN

GOD SPEAKS THROUGH YOU

A PASTOR'S GUILT

There are several aspects of ministry that can cause a pastor to feel guilty.

Chapter 19, page 225, it is stated: "Frank knew plenty of pastors who entered with a call and settled for a profession that soon became a job."

1. What are the pressures that cause clergy to experience the loss of a sense of call?

2. What is the guilt associated with beginning to see your work as just another job?

In Chapter 20, page 238,

"Frank was personally aware of the inherent guilt born by many clergy, conservative and liberal. They frequently judged themselves more harshly than the public. They were charged with proclaiming a gospel of truth yet many pastors felt hypocritical in their inward thoughts and at times in their own behavior."

3. How do pastors manage internal guilt when they recognize failure in their own behavior?

MORE THAN KNOWLEDGE

In speaking to the seminary students in Chapter 22, page 258, Frank tells them,

"Here is the sad truth. Some of you will have your careers, reputation, and even your lives destroyed by an act of sex." There were a few heads nodding in awareness. "That's not because you have used reason and logic to arrive at your decision to act.". . . Whatever makes a person risk everything for a relatively brief physical experience, it is not because that person lacks intelligence. So please don't think you are safe because you are too smart to do such a thing."

4. If most clergy are intelligent people who intellectually understand the price of scandal in their lives, what are the factors that cause them to risk such behavior as having an affair?

5. If knowledge is not enough to protect them from such behavior, what would you suggest are ways to develop such protection?

BEING A WINDOW ONTO THE DIVINE

In Chapter 22, page 259, Frank speaks of the power of ministry and the effect on others of your being a clergy.

"You proclaim a faith of love that is incarnated or fleshed out in the lives of people who interact with each other on a physical basis. Many of those people are desperately lonely, not only for the love of another human being but also for the love of God. However crazy it may seem at the moment, you will represent their closest association with God. Whether you want to or not, you will be their window to the divine.

If you ignore that truth, you will make yourself blind to the powers
that can sneak up on you."

Later Frank expands on the human need inherent in all humans in
Chapter 28, page 339.

"However you interpret the story of Adam and Eve in the garden, it
speaks of the two great voids in a human's life. In the first case, we
are separated from God. We feel the limitations of our finiteness and
yearn to be part of the whole. In the other case, we are separated from
each other. We are not complete without the other, but we also fear
that which is different from us."

6. How do such thoughts affect your understanding of your
    call and the responsibility you have for people with whom
    you relate?

MEETING TWENTY

REFLECTING AND EVALUATING

THEOLOGICAL REFLECTION

As is your practice, settle in for more fun, food, fiction, and fellowship.

1. Allow each person to share some thoughts about what this experience has meant.

2. Include in those reflections how this experience has impacted his or her life as a pastor.

3. Then, go around again and have them speak of what they might suggest for the future.

In addition to the bonds of friendship formed, you also have a pattern for some theological reflection based on stories. This same model can be used to discuss other works of fiction. You can also explore some of the suggestions made available on the Web site of the

Presbytery Pastoral Care Network

www.pastoralcarenetwork.org

Different members can accept the assignment of bringing ideas from either that Web site or the author's Web site, *www.smccutchan.com* for group discussion.

THANK YOU FOR YOUR MINISTRY

Thank you for responding to God's call in your life.

Thank you for all those who are touched by your ministry.

Thank you for caring about yourself and your clergy colleagues.

If I can be of help to you, you may contact me at *steve@smccutchan.com*. The chief end of [all humanity] is to glorify God and enjoy him forever.

APPENDIX

Prayers for the Clergy Based on Selected Psalms

As resources for pastoral support groups, I have included a series of prayers for use by clergy. You are invited to choose a prayer that seems appropriate to the discussion of each meeting. The prayers are either a particular psalm, an adaptation of a psalm, or inspired by the structure of the psalm. You may want to alternate the format between praying in unison or responsively.

You are free to copy these psalm prayers for use in clergy support groups but please identify their source in case others wish to contact me. I will start each of these prayers on a separate page to make it easier to copy them.

Since these prayers and psalm adaptations are my creation, I encourage you to approach them with creativity. If you wish to make further adaptations, feel free to do so.

Much of this work is adapted from my book, *EXPERIENCING THE PSALMS: Weaving the Psalms into Your Ministry and Faith*. More information on this book and other resources for clergy are available on my Web site *www.smccutchan.com*.

1. Confession of Sins for A Company of Pastors

Based on Psalm 51

Call To Confession

To confess our sins is to confess to all those experiences, thoughts, and attitudes that distance us from God and God's purpose in our lives. As our prayer of confession, we will use verses from Psalm 51 adapted to refer directly to each of us.

Prayer of Confession

(May be prayed in unison or by alternating groups.)

Psalm 51

1. Have mercy on [each of us] O God, according to your steadfast love; according to your abundant mercy blot out [our] transgressions.

2. Wash [us] thoroughly from [our] iniquity, and cleanse [us] from [our] sin[s].

3. For [we] know [our] transgressions, and [our sins are] ever before [us].

4. Against you, you alone, [each of us] has sinned, and done what is evil in your sight, so that you are justified in your sentence and blameless when you pass judgment.

5. You desire truth in the inward being; therefore teach [us] wisdom in [our] secret heart.

6. Purge [us] with hyssop, and [we] shall be clean; wash [us], and [we] shall be whiter than snow.

7. Let [us] hear joy and gladness; let the bones that you have crushed rejoice.

8. Hide your face from [our] sins, and blot out all [our] iniquities.

9. Create in [each of us] a clean heart, O God, and put a new and right spirit within [us].

10. Do not cast [us] away from your presence, and do not take your Holy Spirit from [us].

11. Restore to [us] the joy of your salvation, and sustain in [us] a willing spirit.

Assurance of Forgiveness

In the name of Christ, I declare to you, that as we have confessed, so we are forgiven. In the words of that same psalm, the sacrifice that is acceptable to God is a broken spirit and a contrite heart. Come in humility before your Lord and Savior and accept God's forgiveness; God has accepted each and every one of us. Let us rise and give God the glory.

2. Prayers for A Company of Pastors

(A reaffirmation of our faith and calling)
Based on Psalm 1 and 2

Happy are those, God,

Who are not easily tempted by appeals to their selfishness.

Who do not follow the crowd when their direction is wrong.

Who are not impressed by the cynics and skeptics of our age.

Bless those, Lord,

Who will seriously seek to lead a Godly life,

Who will take time to study your Word and your way.

The truly faithful, God, are like trees planted by streams of water

That continue to draw nourishment from your spirit

And produce fruit in their lives that nourishes others.

Why do nations conspire and people engage in endless scheming?

What happens to cause government officials to betray their offices?

Why do some corporate leaders fail in their responsibilities?

Why have some churches strayed from your calling?

What causes people to rebel against the love, justice, and mercy that would reflect their praise of you?

We do not understand the causes of evil, God, but we do affirm our faith in the midst of such a confusing world by lifting our voices in joyful praise for you alone are holy.

---

3.   Prayers for A Company of Pastors

(Expressing our yearning as clergy and churches)
Psalm 15

O Lord, who is worthy to be in your presence,

Who can come into your sanctuary fully confident that they belong here?

We want to be among those whose life is without blame and who always do what is right.

We want to be a people who always speak the truth,

Who never slander with their tongue,

Who never let their friends down,

And who are always honest and caring towards their neighbors.

We want to be a people who always stand up against wickedness,

And who always show honor towards people of faith.

We seek to be a people who are willing to stand by the word of truth even when we suffer for such actions,

A people who generously give to others in need without thought of return,

And who never try to use their position to take advantage of other people.

We seek all these things, Lord, because we know that these are the measures of faith that will hold us in a steady relationship with you.

But when we fail, Lord,

When our fears or lusts overcome our desire to be faithful,

And we come into this sanctuary unworthy of your love,

Let your face shine upon us and be gracious to us.

Fill our hearts with such gratitude that it overflows into our relationships with all we meet.

If we cannot be faithful, Lord, help us to allow you to be faithful through us that all the world might give glory to your name.

4. Prayers for A Company of Pastors

(Prayer of trust in God]
Based on Psalm 25

God, to you we lift up our soul.

We have placed our trust in you.

Do not let us be put to shame or allow the cynics to exult over us.

Do not let those who strive to be faithful be put to shame.

If anyone deserves shame, it is those who mock faith.

Help us to know your ways, O Lord.

Teach us your paths.

Lead this church in your truth and teach us, for you are the God of our salvation.

For you we wait all day long.

Be mindful of your mercy, God, and of your steadfast love for that is what the Scriptures and the faithful have testified to from the beginning.

Do not remember the past sins of our church or even our current transgressions.

Rather, according to your steadfast love, remember us for your goodness sake, O Lord.

For your name's sake, O Lord, pardon our guilt and teach us to revere you.

Turn to us and be gracious to us when we are lonely and afflicted.

Relieve the troubles of our heart and bring us out of our distress.

Take note of any of us who are suffering afflictions or trouble and forgive our sins.

Consider the tremendous challenges we face and the many faces of evil that threaten us.

Guard our lives and deliver us.

Do not let the members of your church be put to shame for in you we have taken refuge.

Allow our integrity and our uprightness to preserve us for we wait for you.

---

5. Remembering God's Faithfulness

Based on Psalm 40

God, we have waited patiently for you.

You have inclined to us and heard when we cried out in distress.

You have drawn us up from many a desolate pit and saved us from the miry bog.

When we have been confused, you have repeatedly set
our feet upon a rock and made our steps secure.

When we remember how faithful you have been to us,
it is like you have put a song in our mouth. We come
this day to sing your praises.

We pray that when others see how faithful you have
been to us, they, too, will put their trust in you.

Blessed are those who place their trust in you, Lord.

Blessed are those who are not trapped by their pride
and pursue false values in this world.

You have multiplied your wondrous deeds on our behalf
and blessed us with countless signs of your presence in
our lives.

Were we to try to count up the many ways that you
have been faithful and kind to us, we would run out
of numbers.

We have spoken of your deliverance in our congregations.

We have refused to keep quiet about your faithfulness.

We have told your story and celebrated your goodness.

Do not, O Lord, withhold your mercy from us.

Let your steadfast love and your faithfulness keep us
safe.

We live in a dangerous world, and the temptations of
our hearts are many.

We can easily be blinded by the glitter of our society.

They are more than the hairs on our heads.

Sometimes our hearts fail us.

Be pleased, O Lord, to deliver us.

Make haste to help us.

Let those who mock the faith be put to shame.

Let those who seek to be clever without God recognize their own confusion.

But may all who seek you rejoice and be glad in you.

May those who love your saving grace sing your praises.

Hear us as we lift up to you the names of the needy among us.

(Lift up their names in silence)

Be their help and deliverer.

Do not delay your healing touch.

---

6. Waiting for God in Times of Turmoil

Based on Psalm 62

God, for you alone our soul waits in silence.

From you comes our salvation.

You are our rock and salvation, our fortress.

Because of you, we will not be shaken.

The world declares to us that violence is acceptable.

People take pleasure in attacking each other.

People rejoice in seeing a person of prominence exposed.

In defense of positions, falsehoods are found acceptable.

Underneath a veneer of pleasantness, the world seethes
with anger.

But we turn to you, the rock of our salvation.

Our hope is in you.

We will trust in you at all times.

We will pour out our heart before you.

You are our refuge.

Even in turmoil, our soul waits for you.

We trust, Lord, that neither disgrace nor fame sways
you.

They are like a breath that soon disappears.

Neither wealth nor poverty buys your love.

When the world comes to an end, your power will still
be present.

When all else has forsaken us, your steadfast love is steady.

For you love your creation and bless those who praise you.

We trust in your healing power.

We pray for this nation as it seeks direction.

We pray for your church as it experiences the anxiety of the future.

We pray for our people who are in need of your healing.

We trust in you at all times,

We pour out our heart to you.

You are our refuge and our strength.

---

7. Prayer of Thanksgiving and Intercession

(Reaffirmation of the core of our faith)
Based on Psalm 127

"Unless the Lord builds the house, those who build it labor in vain."

God, each of us has tried to hold our lives and our families together. We want to build a good life for them. But sometimes, Lord, it feels like life will fall apart.

We know, Lord, that unless you are present with us as

we seek to build our lives, we can easily build an empty
shell. Be present with all the families of our churches.

"Unless the Lord guards the city, the guard keeps watch
in vain."

The nations of the world continue to expend much of
what you have given us either preparing for or engaging
in war.

We struggle for security out of fear, Lord, but often we
fail to consider you in our preparations.

Our own nation is paying the tragic cost of war. God,
show us a better way.

It is in vain that we rise up early and go late to rest,
eating the bread of anxious toil; for God gives sleep to
his beloved.

Lord, our lives are filled with anxiety. We pray that you
might grace us with the gift of sleep for your beloved.

Children are a heritage from the Lord, the fruit of the
womb, a reward. Lord, our families are precious to us.
They are a fragile gift that has been entrusted to us.

Grant us the wisdom to parent them well and the
sensitivity to hear their pains and struggles with love.

God, help us also to be sensitive to all of the other
children of this world who suffer the hunger, violence,
and neglect of a world gone astray.

Grant that in some small way we might be a source of

healing for some of them and that the Body of Christ across the world might reach out to many of them.

Build our house, Lord, our family, our church, our nation, and our world.

Inspire our leaders and enable us to draw on the wisdom of our faith.

---

8. A Prayer for Each of Our Churches

Based on Psalm 67

1 May God be gracious to the church and bless the church and make his face to shine upon the church, Selah

2 that your way may be known upon earth, your saving power among all churches.

3 Let [my church] praise you, O God; let all churches praise you.

4 Let [my church] be glad and sing for joy, for you judge the church with equity and guide all churches upon earth.   Selah

5 Let [my church] praise you, O God; let all the churches praise you.

6 The earth has yielded its increase; God, our God, has blessed us.

7 May God continue to bless our churches so that all humanity may praise God.

9. Prayer Praising the Sovereignty of God

Based on Psalm 90
God, you have been our refuge in all generations.

Sometimes we become so anxious, and then we
remember that before the mountains were brought forth
or ever you had formed the earth and the world, from
everlasting to everlasting, you are God.

You have been there before us, and you will be there in
the end. When we become anxious about the pressure
of time, we remember that a thousand years in our
sight are like a yesterday when it is past or like a watch
in the night.

There are times, Lord, when we feel consumed by your
anger and overwhelmed by the sins of our lives. We
know that you know all our failings that even our most
secret of sins is no secret to you.

We cannot conceive that you could possibly love us or
find our lives a delight.

Then we turn and discover that your wrath is but a
wrath of sorrow. Your heart is wounded by our own
inability to trust your love for us.

Lord, life is too short for us to acquire the wisdom to
know what is good and what is evil.

We live for seventy years, perhaps eighty with good
health, and even then we resent the shortness of life
rather than rejoice in the gift of life.

Teach us to count our days that we might gain wisdom of heart.

We pray that you might allow us to begin each morning filled with your love so that we might rejoice and be glad all our days.

Help us to begin now to rejoice as often as in the past we have been sad.

Let your work be visible in our lives and help our children to be signs of your compassion.

Let your favor be upon us and make our lives beneficial to all who come into contact with us.

10. Prayer in Moments of Despair

Based on Psalm 13

1 How long, O Lord? Will you forget me forever? How long will you hide your face from me?

2 How long must I bear pain in my soul, and have sorrow in my heart all day long? How long shall my enemy be exalted over me?

3 Consider and answer me, O Lord my God! Give light to my eyes, or I will sleep the sleep of death,

4 and my enemy will say, "I have prevailed"; my foes will rejoice because I am shaken.

5 But I trusted in your steadfast love; my heart shall rejoice in your salvation.

6 I will sing to the LORD, because he has dealt bountifully with me.

---

11. Prayer for the Clergy

Based on Psalm 16

Protect your clergy, O God, for in you they take refuge.

The clergy cry out to the Lord in distress: "You are my Lord; I have no good apart from you."

As for the faithful ones in the church, they are the noble, in whom your clergy delight.

Those whose gods are other values multiply their sorrows; their drink offerings of violence your clergy will not honor or offer words of praise upon their lips.

The Lord is your clergy's chosen portion and their cup; you hold their lot.

The boundary lines have fallen for the ordained in pleasant places; they have a goodly heritage.

Faithful clergy bless the Lord who gives them counsel; in the night also their heart instructs them.

They keep the Lord always before them; because God is at their right hand, they shall not be moved.

Because your clergy are called by God, their hearts are glad, and their souls rejoice; their bodies also rest secure.

For you do not give them up to Sheol, or let your faithful ones see the Pit.

You show your clergy the path of life.

In your presence there is fullness of joy; in your right hand are pleasures forevermore.

---

12.   Awaken Your Pastors, God

Based on Psalm 57

1 Be merciful to [clergy], O God, be merciful to [clergy], for in you [clergy's] souls take refuge; in the shadow of your wings, [clergy] will take refuge, until the destroying storms pass by.

2 [The clergy] cry to God Most High, to God who fulfills his purpose through [the clergy].

3 God will send from heaven and save [the clergy], he will put to shame those who trample on [the clergy], Selah

God will send forth his steadfast love and his faithfulness.

4 [The clergy] lie down among lions that greedily devour human prey; their teeth are spears and arrows, their tongues sharp swords.

5 Be exalted, O God, above the heavens. Let your glory be over all the earth.

6 They set a net for [the clergy's] steps; [the clergy's]

souls were bowed down. They dug a pit in [the clergy's] path, but they have fallen into it themselves.   Selah

7 [The clergy's] hearts are steadfast, O God, [the clergy's] hearts are steadfast. [Your pastors] will sing and make melody.

8 Awake, [your pastors'] souls! Awake, O harp and lyre! [Your pastors] will awake the dawn.

9 [Your pastors] will give thanks to you, O Lord, among the peoples; [your pastors] will sing praises to you among the nations.

10 For your steadfast love is as high as the heavens; your faithfulness extends to the clouds.

11 Be exalted, O God, above the heavens. Let your glory be over all the earth.

---

13.   When Gossip Threatens Your Church

Based on Psalm 64

1 Hear my voice, O God, in my complaint; preserve my life from the dread of gossip.

2 Hide me from the secret plots of the gossiper, from the scheming of gossip mongers

3 who whet their tongues like swords, who aim bitter words like arrows,

4 shooting from ambush at the blameless; they shoot suddenly and without fear.

5 They hold fast to their gossiping; they talk of laying snares secretly, thinking, "Who can see us?

6 Who can search out our crimes? We have thought out a cunningly conceived plot." For the human heart and mind are deep.

7 But God will shoot his arrow at them; they will be wounded suddenly.

8 Because of their tongue he will bring them to ruin; all who see them will shake with horror.

9 Then everyone will fear; they will tell what God has brought about, and ponder what he has done.

10 Let the righteous rejoice in the Lord and take refuge in him. Let all the upright in heart glory.

---

14. God Is at the Center of Life

Based on Psalm 1

Happy are those who do not follow the advice of the wicked,

Or take the path that sinners tread,

Or sit in the seat of scoffers;

But their delight is in the [goodness of life].

And on [its promises] they meditate day and night.

They are like trees planted by streams of water

Which yield their fruit in its season,

And their leaves do not wither.

In all they do, they prosper.

The wicked are not so,

But they are like chaff that the wind drives away.

Therefore the wicked will not stand in the judgment,

Nor sinners in the [gathering] of the righteous,

But the way of the wicked will perish.

---

15. Our Thirst for God

Based on Psalm 42-43

As a deer longs for flowing streams, so our souls long for you, O God.

Our souls thirst for God, for the living God.

We remember, as we pour out our souls, how we have gathered as a congregation repeatedly and lifted up our glad shouts and songs of thanksgiving.

Yet, Lord, there are times when all of us have experienced depression in our souls and disquiet in our spirits. At such times we feel distant from you and only cling to a faith that promises that our hope is in God and that we will again praise you.

At such times, we say to you, "God, our rock, why have you forgotten us? Why must we walk about mournfully because tragedy and misfortune oppresses us?"

As with deadly wounds in our bodies, these experiences of doubt, misfortune, and even evil taunt us. At such times we want to cry out, "Where is our God?"

Vindicate us, O God, and defend our cause against the cynicism and doubt of our time.

Deliver us from the deceit and injustice of our time. For you are the God in whom we take refuge.

Send out your light and your truth and let them lead us. Do not let our souls be cast down.

Do not let there be disquiet in our spirits. Let us rise up and praise you to the world around us.

---

16.   God's Grace and the Church

(The interpretation may be incorporated in
the prayer or simply reflected on.)

(Insert the name of your church for FCC)

Psalm 23 (with interpretation)

"The Lord is [First Community Church's] shepherd, [FCC] shall not want."

If it is true, that [FCC] does not lack anything necessary as long as God is shepherding your congregation, what does that say to you about your ministry? Even in times of stress, can you trust God's care of you?

"[God] makes [FCC] lie down in green pastures; [God] leads [FCC] beside still waters: [God] restores [FCC's] soul."

> Look at the ways that God has provided your church with experiences of restoration. Strive to avail yourself of those moments of rest and restoration.

[God] leads [FCC] in right paths for his name's sake.

If God is leading you in right paths, what are some of those paths that beckon to you as a congregation? Where do you feel the nudge of God?

"Even though [FCC] walks through the darkest valley, [FCC] fears no evil; for you are with [FCC]; your rod and your staff—they comfort [FCC]."

> Let the pastors review some of the dark moments in their history and upon reflection how they have been both prodded (the rod) and rescued (the staff) from those experiences. Does that past history provide them some comfort and strength that they are not alone in their journey?

"[God] prepares a table before [FCC] in the presence of [FCC's] enemies; God anoints [FCC's] head with oil; [FCC's] cup overflows."

> All churches have negative experiences or opposition that acts like an enemy to their practice of the faith. Sometimes it is people, or the values of society, or conditions that surround the congregation. It may even be a negative spirit among some of the members. Yet even in the midst of such experiences, there have been moments of joy and celebration. It might be a liturgical event, like Easter, or it may be a birthday of an elderly member that is recognized. Maybe it is just a good church picnic in which they enjoy the pleasures of eating

and fellowshipping together. Whatever it is, how have they allowed those experiences to interrupt the power of negativity and reminded them of the joy of faith?

"Surely goodness and mercy shall follow [FCC] all the days of her life, and [FCC] shall dwell in the house of the Lord her whole life long."

God has been with you at the beginning of your journey as a faith community and will be with you at the end. How can you affirm that faith as a congregation?

---

17   The Center of the Church

(Not a Psalm but powerful to pray this way.)
(May be prayed in unison or in alternating parts.)

1 CORINTHIANS 13 FOR CLERGY AND CONGREGATIONS

If clergy speak in the tongues of mortals and of angels, but congregations do not have love, clergy are noisy gongs and congregations are clanging cymbals.

And if clergy have prophetic powers, and congregations understand all mysteries, and clergy have all knowledge, and congregations have all faith, so as to remove mountains, but do not have love, both clergy and congregations are nothing.

If congregations give away all their possessions, and clergy hand over their bodies so that they may boast, but neither have love, they gain nothing.

Clergy love is patient; congregational love is kind.

Clergy love is not envious or boastful or arrogant, and congregational love is not rude.

Loving clergy do not insist on their own way nor are loving congregations irritable or resentful; loving clergy do not rejoice in wrongdoing but rejoice in the truth.

Congregational love bears all things; loving clergy believes all things; loving congregations hope all things; and loving clergy endures all things.

Love among clergy and congregations never ends. But as for prophecies, they will come to an end; as for tongues, they will cease; as for knowledge, it will come to an end.

For congregations know only in part, and clergy prophesy only in part; but when the complete comes, the partial will come to an end.

When clergy and congregations first begin, they speak like children, think like children, and reason like children, but when clergy and congregations mature, they put an end to childish ways.

For congregations and clergy see in a mirror, dimly, but in time will see face to face.

Each knows only in part; then they will know fully, even as they have been fully known.

And for both clergy and congregations, faith, hope, and love abide, these three; and the greatest of these is love.

A FINAL WORD FROM STEVE MCCUTCHAN

It is not easy to be engaged in pastoral ministry in our society. It is important to keep in mind that the better pastor you are, the more demanding your ministry will be. This book is intended to encourage you to build a network of support for yourself and to be part of offering this to other clergy as well.

The *Healthy Clergy Make Healthy Congregations* series is intended to provide you some needed resources to undergird your ministry. It rests on the belief that the best ministry is done in concert with others who are also called to the ministry. We need each other, and we need to be responsive to the issues that our colleagues face as well.

In addition to this book, I have provided a book *An Interim Pastor's Gift* that offers suggestions for interim pastors to educate a congregation in ways to be supportive of their clergy. When interims advocate for clergy care, they are not advocating for themselves but for the congregation and the future clergy.

A third book in the series *God Laughs—Why Don't You?* explores the value of comedy and humor in coping with the stresses of ministry. While ministry is serious business, it is best done with a sense of humor. Humor makes us more flexible and adaptive, and it helps us to remember that we are not the savior. While our skills and gifts are important, our hope is in God.

Additional resources are identified on the following page. Also, I encourage you to explore what is available at the Presbytery Pastoral Care Network Web site *www.pastoralcarenetwork.org*. You are invited to attend one of our annual conferences and connect with others who share your passion for the care of clergy. See the Web site for further information *www.pastoralcarenetwork.org*.

RESOURCES BY STEPHEN McCUTCHAN

WWW.SMCCUTCHAN.COM

HEALTHY CLERGY MAKE HEALTHY CONGREGATIONS

A Company of Pastors: Overcoming Isolation	Amazon
Clergy Tales—Tails (3 Volumes)	Amazon
A Star & A Tear (mystery novel)	*Amazon*
An Interim Pastor's Gift	Amazon
God Laughs—Why Don't You?	Amazon

THE WATER SERIES (A devotional series based on the Revised *Common Lectionary*)

Water From the Well	(Year A)	CSS pub
Streams of Living Water	(Year B)	CSS pub
Water From the Rock	(Year C)	CSS pub

BIBLICAL RESOURCES

Experiencing the Psalms	Smyth & Helwys
Good News for a Fractured Society	Author House

CDS DESIGNED FOR SUPPORT OF PASTORS

A Deep Well for the Pastor	*www.smccutchan.com*
Laughter From the Well	*www.cdbaby.com*

COMMUNITY ISSUES

Let's Have Lunch	Amazon